Life on the Dole

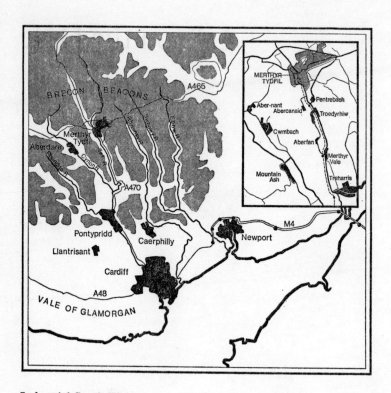

Industrial South Wales

Mervyn Jones

Life on the Dole

Davis-Poynter

First Published by Davis-Poynter Limited
Broadwick House Broadwick Street London W1V 2AH

Copyright © 1972 by Mervyn Jones

ISBN 0 7067 0035 X

Printed in Great Britain by
Bristol Typesetting Company Limited
Barton Manor St Philips Bristol

'People should keep unemployment figures in perspective . . . There is an enormous obsession with unemployment. It is all too easy to talk oneself into a position of gloom and despondency.'

–Sir John Eden, Minister for Industry, speaking at Sheffield on 27 September 1971

Life on the Dole

Part One | The Town

1

The day began dank and chilly. A heavy white mist clutched the town, hung motionless in the narrow streets, and made the surrounding hills invisible. It was October 30, 1971; in most of the country it was just another Saturday, but in Merthyr Tydfil it was the day for the demonstration against unemployment, under the slogan of 'The Right to Work'. There hadn't been any demonstrations in Merthyr, whether on this theme or another, for a good many years, and there are no professional marchers – no Rentacrowd – here, so the turnout would depend largely on the weather. We had been keeping our fingers crossed all the week, for the west winds can carry clouds smack into the mountains; Merthyr's annual rainfall total is double that of London and much of it comes down in the autumn. Five years ago almost to a day, torrential rain had set the old coal-tip sliding and made Aberfan, a couple of miles away along the narrow valley of the Taf, into a name for horror.

But the fine autumn weather of 1971 held. Between ten o'clock and half past, as the marchers gathered in Swan Street, the mist began to disperse; and at noon, when they were going up the steep path through Cyfarthfa Park, those who had come in overcoats were sweating under a warm sun, with the hills now clear and the rich colours of the trees – oak and maple and sycamore and the national mountain ash – brilliant against the blue sky.

'Back to the Thirties? No!' said several of the placards carried on the march. Among the older people, there was grave talk of the days of mass unemployment and the Hunger Marches. It was thirty-five years since King Edward

VIII, or the Prince of Wales as he is better remembered, had come to see crowds of workless men in Merthyr and departed from royal protocol to say 'Something must be done for these people'. A woman in Swan Street remembered it well; she had been a housemaid in London, like many another Welsh girl, but had been at home when the King came. She was reminded of it, now in 1971, because another Prince of Wales was due to visit Merthyr in a few days' time. 'I wonder what he'll have to say,' she remarked. As to what Edward VIII had said, her comment was: 'They got rid of him smartly after that.' *They* were the ruling class, the authorities, the Tories, the people for whom unemployment is an abstract problem about which one shouldn't get too much obsessed. Ineradicable in South Wales is the belief that the King's words about unemployment, not his matrimonial intentions, were the reason for his being 'got rid of'.

The present Prince of Wales, as it turned out, was seen by few people because of the security precautions (which were not considered so necessary in 1936) and is not recorded to have said anything about unemployment. In fact, he came to Merthyr to make a speech about pollution and congratulate young volunteers on tidying up the banks of the Taf. For much has changed, certainly, since the years before the war. We must keep things in proportion, as we are often told; Merthyr's unemployment figure on the day of the demonstration was 6.6%, not 63% as in the trough of the depression. Most of the marchers were in decent suits or tweed jackets, the youngsters in patterned shirts, the girls in mini-skirts and fashionable leather boots. Oxfam enthusiasts had taken advantage of the gathering and most of the marchers had paid for paper flags reading 'Freedom from Hunger'; the time when the hunger that concerned people in Merthyr was their own was an age away. If one of the thousands of men who left Merthyr to seek work elsewhere in the 'thirties had returned for this demonstration, he would have recognized nothing in Swan Street but the old Swan Inn. The modern office building belonging to the Amalgamated Union of Engineering Workers (a union with very few members here until the war, but now Merthyr's largest); the palatial police station across the street; the bright new primary school in whose playground the march formed up; the shopping precinct nearby; the suburban-looking houses and flats built by the Council on the site of old slums; the imposing College of Further Education across the Taf – all these would be strange to him.

Yet, when all this is said, unemployment is what the demonstration was about, just as much as the Hunger Marches were. People were priding themselves on their peaceful and orderly protest – not like those riotous affairs in London that they'd seen on television – but their mood was anxious, determined, deeply concerned and not without an edge of bitterness. Merthyr had been promised that unemployment would not return, and the promise had been broken. *They* were once again indifferent, and *they* must be made to listen. In the speeches made in Cyfarthfa Park, by the Mayor and the Rector and Professor Brinley Thomas and Michael Foot, that was the note which won the response of cheers.

The march was a serious affair, then; but it was not gloomy. Five bands played anything from 'Men of Harlech' to 'When the Saints Come Marching In'. The huge colourful banners from the union branches and miners' lodges were there, one of them with a portrait of Keir Hardie, Merthyr's MP from 1900 to his death in 1915. There were pretty girls, and mothers pushing prams, and students with their long scarves. The demonstration had been sponsored by the Council of Churches as well as the Labour Party and the unions, so there were Baptist ministers and Catholic priests and clergy of the Church of Wales. And there were marchers with home-made placards to remind us that unemployment is a personal matter for the unemployed as well as a social problem. One of them read: 'Dunkirk – 5 years PoW – Now the Dole'. Another, carried by a five-year-old girl, read: 'My Grandpa Wants Work'.

As we left the modern housing estate behind, the landmarks would have been more familiar to the returned emigrant. The ornate fountain and cupola, a masterpiece of Victorian ironwork, which commemorates 'Robert and Lucy Thomas of Waunwyllt in this parish, the pioneers in 1828 of the South Wales steam coal trade'. The old church of St Tydfil, now closed except for occasional musical events. (Merthyr means 'martyr'; Tydfil was a premature Christian slaughtered by pagans a generation before the conversion of the Welsh.) Then the High Street, still narrow and winding as it climbs out of the valley. The ABC cinema, still spoken of as the Castle, built for the age before television when going to the pictures on Saturday night was the almost universal escape from reality. The stone-built public library, which a determined Council somehow managed to give to the town in the depression years. The Town Hall, a formidable red-brick structure with thick walls and narrow windows, referred to as the Kremlin; Merthyr may not have much in common with Moscow, but it does have half a century of single-party rule. The Employment Exchange – a pretty important place, this – at the street junction impressively entitled Pontmorlais Circus, where the march turns sharp left at the only traffic light in the borough. Bethesda Street, named after one of its several chapels; like most Welsh towns, Merthyr has every imaginable place of Christian worship from Seventh Day Adventist to Mormon, and unlike most Welsh towns it has a synagogue too. Brecon Road, still lined with houses of unfaced stone whose front doors lead straight into the living-room. Finally the park, and the march becomes a meeting on the broad esplanade in front of Cyfarthfa Castle.

The history of the castle will tell you a good deal about Merthyr. Cyfarthfa means 'barking', and it's believed that someone kept hunting dogs here – they would have hunted deer, not foxes – when Merthyr was a village. But in 1765 the Cyfarthfa ironworks came to make the Taf dirty and the sky smoky. Anthony Bacon, the original ironmaster, sold out to a hard-headed and hard-driving Yorkshireman named Richard Crawshay. The Crawshays became a dynasty, and it was the third of the line who built himself a castle in 1825. The barons of industry in those days didn't think of living far from the works; the castle, on the slope of quite a small hill, dominated the scene of enrichment and the huddled cottages of the workers from close quarters, and the servants must have been kept busy cleaning the grime from the windows. Nevertheless it is a real castle, not merely a residence or a mansion. Built in the style of a medieval fortress, it has battlements, fifteen rounded towers, and stone walls that might have resisted even the cannon that the Crawshays made for the Napoleonic Wars. It also has 72 rooms and 365 windows, one for every day of the year. It cost £30,000, which was worth about eight times what it is today. The expense may be partly accounted for by the fact that the young master, who wanted the place ready for his bride, insisted on getting it built within a year. This Crawshay had invested in the West Indies trade and other lines of business, and one authority says that he was the richest man in Britain, though probably others could have contested the title. However, the bulk of the £30,000 must have been produced by the labours of Merthyr miners and ironworkers.

At the time when the castle was built, the family of one of Crawshay's workers would have lived in a single-storey cottage, comprising not 72 rooms but two, each room measuring eight by ten feet. There might have been a couple of lodgers, unmarried men newly arrived from the Cardigan farms or off the boat from Ireland, whose living-space was a cot in the corner. Almost certainly the bed would have been used by children as well as by mother and father. Families were large because the replacement rate was high; infants died at birth more often than not, toddlers died quickly of cholera and measles and dysentery, young workers of eight years of age died before they'd learn to avoid accidents in the mines. Taking one hazard with another, the average Merthyr baby had an expectation of 17 years of life. A man worked 84 hours a week – dawn to dark most days of the year, Sundays included – and earned one pound for it, more or less: thirty shillings as the top rate at the iron furnaces, ten shillings for a labourer. Women hauling tubs in the pits got six shillings, children two or three. Bread was a halfpenny for a good round Welsh loaf, but all the same the family earnings were a small slice of the profits that built Cyfarthfa Castle.

All that is long ago. Yet something in the collective memory of this town recalls not only the 1930s, but the 1830s too. In the age of the 40-hour week, the modern Council house, the refrigerator and the washing-machine, three facts remain. One: this is a town where men and women earn money by real work, in pay-packets measured from Friday to Friday, and not by any kind of easy option. Two: the availability of work depends on conditions shaped far away, on 'the state of trade' as it was called in Crawshay's time or the 'macro-economic factors' as contemporary jargon has it, and the shadow on the sunniest day is always unemployment. Three: whatever wealth is made in Merthyr, a hefty slice goes to directors and shareholders and investing banks. Crawshay's successors would go unrecognized in Merthyr streets, and live in West End flats rather than in castles, but they exist.

So the castle is a monument, a survival from the past; and this obscures the truth that it is also a significant reminder. The Cyfarthfa ironworks closed down in 1920. Long before that, however, the Crawshay family had found the banks of the Thames more salubrious than those of the Taf and gone to live at Caversham. The castle stood empty behind padlocked gates and the grass grew tall in the park. In 1909, a year after Merthyr became a county borough with power to levy and spend rates, the Council bought it for the bargain price – considering what it had cost to build –

of £18,000. The park became public; half of the castle was turned into a museum and art gallery, the other half into a grammar school. That is how it is used today, except that the school is part of a comprehensive.

So there we were, on the esplanade of Cyfarthfa Castle, listening to Michael Foot while the children clambered on to the cannon which the third Crawshay had mounted as symbols of his industry. It was here, or just down the hill, that Merthyr had helped to make Britain the workshop of the world; it was here that enterprises like Cyfarthfa had gone from zenith to decline, leaving the heritage of an ailing economy and unemployment. The demonstration, in these fitting surroundings, had gone off as planned, had made its point, had presumably been a success. But a few evenings before, when I had met the organizers in the bar of the Miners' Hall, they had confidently predicted that there would be three thousand marchers if the weather held. In the event, not more than one thousand marched. The pavements along the High Street were packed with sympathetic watchers; however, when march stewards with megaphones exhorted them to join in, they contented themselves with smiling and perhaps waving to marchers whom they happened to know. Yet concern over unemployment is the concern of Merthyr, of a town that is emphatically a community. How was this?

One could say simply that unemployment was at 6.6% and not ten times as much. An unemployed engineer, whom I met on the march and later visited at home, told me that he wouldn't have gone along if he hadn't been demonstrating for himself. One could say that there are other things to do on a fine Saturday, in Merthyr as elsewhere. One could recall that demonstrating is an interrupted tradition. But I think there is another reason. The rise in unemployment that has hit Merthyr in recent years is still regarded with a certain incredulity. It contradicts so many plans and promises and guarantees, so many assumptions about what is fitting in modern times – assumptions that seemed to be accepted even by capitalists, even by Tories – that there is a tendency to feel that it cannot be allowed to go on, that 'something will be done'. Yes, there is anxiety; yes, there is some bitterness; but there is not yet anger.

This is to say that *they* still have time. *They* can keep down the excitement, take the necessary measures – I shall discuss later what these could be – and prove eventually that what has been happening was a temporary difficulty, not to be exaggerated either in gravity or in duration. But, as I write this book in the winter of 1971-2, the feeling grows that *they* do not have much time. Anger will rise in Merthyr, and in not a few places like Merthyr. Unemployment can again become the critical issue of politics that it was in the 'thirties.

Meanwhile, for those who are remote from Merthyr, there is in a double sense a task of understanding. It is necessary to understand what is happening to thousands of our fellow-citizens. With this aim, I shall go on in the second half of this book to translate the abstraction called unemployment into individual terms, into life on the dole. But first it is necessary to understand how the present situation has come about: what fissures and failures in the British economy have led to it. The story is neither short nor simple. It goes back for decades and even centuries. It is the story of British capitalism, exemplified almost to scientific perfection in what has happened to Merthyr Tydfil.

2

History is geography with people in it. South Wales, one of Britain's major industrial regions for the last two hundred years, offers particularly clear evidence that man has to work and prosper where the lie of the land allows him. The scene is visible and the history is an easy deduction as you travel along the Heads of the Valleys Road (A 465) which was improved and realigned half a dozen years ago to pass outside, instead of through, places like Merthyr Tydfil.

From Abergavenny, in the valley of the Usk, the road climbs steeply on to a plateau. It will remain a thousand or more feet above sea level for twenty-five miles, until it snakes down the Vale of Neath to reach the coastal basin between Swansea and Port Talbot. On your right, as you go westward, is the massif of the Black Mountains; the central part of this is called the Brecon Beacons, is a national park (its boundary touches that of the borough of Merthyr) and contains some of the most splendid unspoiled countryside in Britain. Economically, there is nothing much up here except forestry, scattered sheep farms, and an occasional quarry. But on your left, rivers whose sources are in the Black Mountains cut steep-sided valleys – hence the name of the road – as they rush down to the flat country called the Vale of Glamorgan. You pass one roundabout junction after another, and each road to the left leads into a valley: the valley of the Ebbw, of the Sirhowy, of the Rhymney, of the Taf, of the Cynon, of the Rhondda. Should you take one of these roads leading south, you will drive between collieries, factories and close-packed rows of houses all the way to the Vale. There are towns in some of the valleys – Tredegar on the Sirhowy, Merthyr on the Taf,

Aberdare on the Cynon – but more characteristically there are strings of swollen industrial and mining villages, grouped administratively into urban districts. The land in these valleys, and between them, is simply made of coal.

The habitable part of a valley is sometimes only a mile wide, seldom more than three or four. Directly behind the houses, the mountains rise. These mountains, dividing one valley from the next, are open moorland, just as empty as the national park. While humanity is teeming down below, the only life on the mountains is animal – flocks of sheep, though not nearly so many as a generation ago, and wild ponies. Each road entering a town has a cattle-grid, but the ponies have their own routes, and when I parked my car at night fifty yards off Merthyr's High Street I sometimes saw a pony nibbling at a patch of grass, as secure and un-disturbed as a sacred cow in Calcutta.

But if you walk over the mountains, you will see that they have been combed for coal over and over again. The coal lies so near the surface that, two hundred years after its ex-ploitation began, there is still an opencast coal site on Merthyr Mountain. For some decades, in the earlier phase of the industrial revolution, there were no pits but only drift mines, which are tunnels driven into the flank of a hill. Anyone could get coal by 'patching' – marking out a patch of land, digging a hole, putting the good coal into a cart or a wheelbarrow, and dumping the slag alongside. Friends or families did it, founding small businesses which sometimes grew but mostly failed, and unemployed men did it to scratch a living in the depression years, selling a bag of coal for one shilling and threepence. As a man worked below ground, he usually had a friend or a boy waiting in the open to prevent the coal from being stolen. The uncle of a man I know in Merthyr employed his dog for this purpose; but one evening the dog came home alone – the do-it-yourself mine had fallen in, as quite often happened. Nowadays, as you wander across the mountains, you notice at times that the ground is broken into hillocks, black under the grass, which are the little slag-heaps made by 'patching'. And sometimes, as you gaze at the view, a much larger hill surprises you by its regular outline and you realise that – although covered by grass, bracken or even trees – it is a coal-tip.

The Heads of the Valleys Road, running across the bare uplands, reaches its fifth roundabout at the outskirts of Merthyr. If you follow the Merthyr signpost, you are at the top of what becomes the High Street. The top end is 800 feet higher above the sea than the lower end on the bank of the Taf, and there are not many High Streets of which this can be said. Going down, you are close beside a stream called the Morlais, which gets lost in sewers like other urban brooks but ends up in the Taf. There used to be an iron bridge over the Morlais called Waterloo Bridge, because it was built in the year of Waterloo, but it is no longer there.

Merthyr, strictly defined – as strictly as London could be limited to the City of London – is on a shelf of land on the left bank of the Taf. The borough of Merthyr is a great deal larger. The citizens put up a long fight to get borough status, the official requirement being a population of 50,000 which to Merthyr's fury was raised to 75,000 halfway through the struggle. Even at the appalling density that was allowed in the nineteenth century, there was nothing like enough room for so many people in Merthyr proper. Consequently, there are two parts to the borough, though the built-up area is continuous. The first group of neighbourhoods includes Merthyr itself and a number of villages – Dowlais and Penydarren higher up the Morlais, Georgetown around the old Cyfarthfa works, Gellideg and Heolgerrig on the other side of the Taf – which have become part of Merthyr as villages like Highgate have become part of London. In this group it's logical to put the village of Cefn Coed, which is officially in the county of Brecon (Merthyr being in Glamorgan) but is sensibly classed with Merthyr for employment statistics. Also in this group are some modern housing estates on high ground around the town, such as Gurnos and Galon Uchaf. The second group consists of villages lower down the Taf – Pentrebach, Troedirhiw, Aberfan, Merthyr Vale, Quaker's Yard (the yard being a graveyard), Treharris and others. The Taf valley is thickly populated all the way from Cardiff up to Merthyr – twenty-five miles by road – and the Merthyr borough boundary comes nine miles from the town itself. The villages in this group have a distinctive identity; a man who lives there is likely to say that his home is near Merthyr, rather than in Merthyr. As we shall see, the industrial history of these villages has been distinctive too.

Merthyr is about as hilly as Rome, and it is rare indeed to walk a hundred yards on level ground anywhere in the borough. Some of the streets are so steep that each little house has a roof-line higher than its neighbour; cars go up in bottom gear and you wonder how the women who live at the top can possibly make it with their prams. The various hills command spectacular views, each of them different. The surrounding mountains, of course, can be seen from practically anywhere. Some of the hills in the outskirts, as I've said, are coal-tips, and one is a slag-heap of a different kind. This is the White Tip – dazzlingly white on a sunny day – made of blast-furnace slag from the Dowlais steelworks, which was in business from 1850 to 1930. This amazing phenomenon dominates Merthyr as Table Mountain dominates Cape Town, and is roughly the same shape; it ends in a sheer cliff about a hundred feet high. The pieces of slag, being made of coke and iron ore consumed by fire, are hard and shiny; their colours – ochrered and sea-green and jet-black – are fascinating. Contractors have started to clear away the tip for use as hard-core in building motorways. The job is expected to take twenty years or more. Many people in Merthyr think that the White Tip ought to be left alone; no other town that I know of has anything like it. Strange it certainly is, beautiful perhaps, and decidedly a monument to Merthyr's past.

Outsiders regard Merthyr as 'a horrible industrial town',

and one must admit that it doesn't look like Bath or Canterbury. It has had a bad name since Carlyle called it 'the squalidest, ugliest place on earth'. These adjectives were merited partly by the housing conditions, which were appalling until fairly recently, and partly by the pall of smoke that hung permanently over the town, the chimneys of the ironworks and steelworks being reinforced by those of thousands of domestic coal-fires. Today there is no pall of smoke, the slums have mostly gone, and the old houses that remain are likely to have preservation orders placed on them now that we look at Victorian building with favour. They stand in neat rows, their proportions are perfect, and they are scrupulously kept; whether the big rough blocks of stone are left bare, or plastered and painted in bright colours in the Welsh tradition, they are infinitely more attractive than anything you'd see in affluent suburbia. Both because of this style of building and because of the spectacular landscape, I'll risk incredulity and say that Merthyr is a beautiful town. What is beyond argument is that the people who live there are proud of it. They want to go on living there – and that means making a living.

3

Suitably enough, it was in the notable year of 1759 that the history of Britain and the history of Merthyr began to move together. 1759 was called the Year of Victories, and inspired a patriotic poet to write the ballad 'Hearts of Oak', which begins:

Come cheer up, my lads, 'tis to glory we steer
To add one more toast to this wonderful year,

During the wonderful year, British sailors smashed the French fleet at Quiberon; British troops, allied with Prussians, defeated the French army at Minden; Wolfe stormed Quebec; other naval forces took Guadeloupe in the West Indies and Pondicherry in India. Though Guadeloupe and Pondicherry were given back by the peace treaty, the war ensured that Britain and not France would become the dominant imperial power both in the Caribbean and in the Indian sub-continent. The profits of the West Indies trade – slaves being shipped one way, sugar and rum the other – and the plunder of India created the financial resources to turn Britain into the first, and for a long time the greatest, of industrial nations.

But a victory of another kind was being won on the mountains of Wales. A man named Lewis had observed that these mountains were rich both in coal and iron ore. He got the idea that iron, for which there was a steadily growing demand, could be made by smelting with coal instead of with charcoal (or burnt wood) as had been done, in the Taf valley as well as in many other places, in the past. He asked for a lease of two thousand acres of land at Dowlais, a couple of miles from the village of Merthyr. The land was practically valueless agriculturally; Lady Windsor, who owned it, granted the lease at £28 a year. (She may have suspected that Lewis was on to something, for the previous lease had been at £26.) In 1847, when the lease ran out, it was to be renewed at £30,000.

Lewis himself knew nothing about iron-smelting. He looked for a man to join with him as junior partner and active manager, and the man he found was John Guest of Broseley in Shropshire. Shropshire, if anywhere, can claim to be the cradle of the industrial revolution; Broseley is a couple of miles from Ironbridge, so called because it has the first iron bridge in the world. Guest, a man of farming stock, had begun to branch out into the embryonic iron business.

He accepted Lewis's proposition and arrived at Dowlais in 1759, riding a sturdy mare with his servant, Ben, riding pillion when the going was rough across the roadless countryside. He didn't take his wife and children with him, and he is said to have made his will before leaving. Going to wild Wales in those days was more like emigration than settling in the flourishing colonies of Virginia or Massachusetts. For a penny a week and sixpence at Christmas, a little girl tramped up from the last post-house on the road to bring John Guest his weekly English paper, more out of date than a Ceylon tea-planter's airmail *Daily Telegraph* would be nowadays.

But Lewis's hunch was right. Only six years after Guest, another English ironmaster followed suit at Cyfarthfa, and the eighteenth century saw the foundation of two more iron-works: the Plymouth works, beside the Taf a stone's throw from what is now the centre of Merthyr, and the Peny-darren works just down the hill from Dowlais. The iron-masters, though competitors, were on friendly terms – a little club of Englishmen among natives speaking a strange language, like early settlers in Africa. Financially, there was plenty of room for the four of them as the market grew and grew again. Iron was needed for bridges and other construction work; for machines, as the textile industry began its whirlwind boom; and for cannon and muskets, for Britain was rarely at peace until after Waterloo. Guest was able to buy out his partner and hand on a substantial business to his son. The firm of Guest, Keen & Nettlefold is in Merthyr to this day, though it is in many other places too.

The ironworks, and the early coal-mines which provided the fuel, demanded labour insatiably. It came, as it always comes in the primary stage of industrialization, from the farms; Welshmen flocked in from half a dozen mountainous and impoverished counties. The population of Merthyr was put at 500 in 1767; it topped 8,000 when the first British census was taken in 1801, and 22,000 in 1831. Merthyr was the biggest town in Wales, and at one time it could have been called the only town in Wales. People to this day are fond of saying: 'We had a town when Cardiff was a fishing village'. Up to the 1861 census, Merthyr stayed in first place; only in the latter half of the nineteenth century was it gradually overtaken by Cardiff, Swansea and Newport.

The employers, and what we should now call the technologists, were English; so were the few tradesmen and professional people. Some of the workers came from Ireland; there has always been an Irish element in Merthyr's population and the name of the present Mayor is Gerry Donovan, though he speaks as if it were Evans or Jones. It is sometimes said that the Catholic Irish had to be brought in because the Nonconformist Welsh wouldn't work on Sundays, but this is probably a legend, for the seven-day week was normal until well into the nineteenth century. (In 1837 Sir John Josiah Guest claimed that his furnaces were the only ones in Merthyr that were banked on Sundays; he was on good terms with the Nonconformist ministers and had recently become Merthyr's first MP with their support.) The Irish influx has been exaggerated by some accounts, and in 1840 the population was recorded as 91%

Welsh. Welsh, too, was the language of the people until the beginning of the twentieth century.

Merthyr people, however, are proud of living in a cosmopolitan town. During the nineteenth century, when 'colonial' ironworks had been established in Spain and Italy, workmen from those countries came to settle in Merthyr. A few street-names show that they had their own districts and for a while they formed distinct communities, though their descendants are now as Welsh as Gerry Donovan. A plaque in the Town Hall commemorates the six local men killed in the last war, and one of the names is Angelo Benito Solari. Strolling round the town, I noted Zanelli's café in the High Street, Ali and Zafar's bargain clothing shop in the market, and Dr Mazumdar's surgery in Church Street between J. Chang's fish-and-chip shop and Liu's Chinese food to take away (is this what happened to Liu Shao-Chi?) There is a striking absence, nevertheless, of the recent Commonwealth immigration that Enoch Powell is so worried about. It is a long time since Merthyr was a town in which immigrants could hopefully look for work.

Back in the early boom years, when Crawshay cannon were booming at Assaye and Badajoz, the prosperity of the iron industry seemed to be limitless. Yet there was a cloud on the horizon. Transport, the problem that companies cite to this day when urged to build their factories at Merthyr, was a difficulty from the start. In the early days, before the railways, there was no question of shifting Merthyr's production eastward through Abergavenny, and the natural outlet was down the valley to Cardiff – Merthyr, in fact, can take the credit for making Cardiff more than a fishing village. The first Guest and the first Crawshay had to move loads of iron down the winding road on the backs of mules or in carts, but this was a slow and inefficient business. The solution found by the ironmasters was the building of a canal; in the Midlands and elsewhere, canals had proved vital in the process of industrialization and inland trade. But, because of the steepness of the Taf valley, the canal needed fifty locks on the twenty-five miles to Cardiff. It was a masterpiece of canal-building, but it was relatively slow and inefficient too.

Samuel Homfray, the ironmaster of Penydarren, decided that he could find the answer. He commissioned a Cornish engineer named Trevithick to lay rails and design a steam tram to run from Penydarren to a point lower down the canal and bypass a number of locks. Richard Crawshay, watching sceptically, bet Homfray £1000 that the tram wouldn't succeed in carrying a ten-ton load of iron. On the appointed day, their employees were given time off work and the whole town turned out to see the marvel. The tram worked, but its tall chimney-stack, made of bricks, hit a bridge, smashing both the bridge and itself. Trevithick had to repair the chimney on the spot; he did it in five hours and Homfray won the bet. He was a little less triumphant the following day when it turned out that the engine lacked the power to haul the empty tubs uphill again. However, this was rectified and the tram went into service. It was a great achievement for 1803, thirty-three years before Stephenson's Rocket. It was, in fact, the first use of steam power for transport in the world. Streets in Merthyr and in some villages down the valley are still called Tram-roadside. Deservedly, there is also a Trevithick Street, although Trevithick's statue has somehow vanished from its pedestal.

With the coming of the railway age, Merthyr's transport anxieties appeared to be over. The Taff Vale Railway (the second 'f' is an Englishman's error) carried iron down to Cardiff at unheard-of speed. Competing companies rushed to get in on the Merthyr trade; there was a rival line on the other side of the Taf, and lines going east to Abergavenny, north to Brecon, west to Swansea. Except the original Taff Vale line, all of these have now been closed. At one period five railway companies operated in Merthyr, but they were merged into the Great Western Railway.

For seventy years after John Guest rode to Dowlais,

Merthyr's business was iron and nothing but iron. Thousands of men were working as miners – or colliers as they were always called in Wales – but the coal was used as fuel for the foundries. It was in 1828, as the monument which I have mentioned recalls, that Robert and Lucy Thomas pioneered the mining of coal to be sold as a commodity in its own right. (Robert died and Lucy carried on the business, a rare effort for a woman in those days.)

The outcome was a boom that eclipsed even the iron boom of the earlier period. The Taff Vale Railway transported 41,000 tons of coal in 1841, 594,000 tons in 1850, and 2,133,000 tons in 1860. Britain was on the verge of becoming the workshop of the world; the industrial revolution, at first largely concentrated on textiles, was bursting into heavy engineering, the metal trades, shipbuilding, and a hundred other branches of production. Coal, now that steam-power had superseded water-power, was needed in factories from Birmingham up to Dundee. Coal was needed by the railways that soon covered the country, and by the steamships (their sides flanked by Merthyr iron) that were ousting the sailing clippers. Coal was needed in the homes of a growing population, especially in the fireplaces swept by a million housemaids and the stoves on which a legion of cooks prepared massive meals. And coal was exported to countries trying to follow Britain on the path to industrialization: to France, whose demands exceeded the output of her own mines, and to Italy where there were no coal resources at all. In 1840 an enterprising Welshman named John Nixon loaded a ship with Merthyr coal at Cardiff and took it to Nantes; he came back with the contract for the French Navy. The Royal Navy was soon buying from the same source, for Welsh coal was recognised as the world's best, with the Pennsylvania product (mined mostly by Welsh emigrants at that time) as the only possible rival. To keep up the reputation, only the best coal was put on the market. Anything else that came out of the mines was thrown aside, to form the tips that still bulk large in the landscape.

Cardiff now became the distribution point for coal from the valleys. It was carried by the main railway line to London, it was loaded into ships for export, and it was used as bunker fuel by the ships themselves. With the development of the West Wales anthracite fields, Swansea too became a fast-growing port. Inland, an entire stretch of South Wales from Monmouthshire across to Carmarthenshire was being transformed into an industrial region.

About Merthyr, two facts must be borne in mind. The demand for coal was turning all the Welsh valleys into strings of densely populated towns and villages. But for most of them – the Rhondda is typical – the change came about only at the period which this narrative has now reached: the railway age, the mid-century high noon of Victorian economic expansion. Merthyr had already been a centre of industry for eighty years. As in so much else, it was first in the field. But already, it was beginning to age. The mines, the industrial equipment, the houses were eighty years old and looked like it.

Secondly, Merthyr itself was not a mining town. When coal became a commodity and extraction began on a large scale the requirement was for deep pits in place of the old drift-mines and tunnels. For geological reasons – mainly because the seams were thicker – these had to be lower down the Taf valley. John Nixon opened up the Merthyr Vale pit, about six miles from the town; it was in its heyday the world's biggest coal-mine, its reserves are colossal, and it is still being worked today. The villages along the valley, though they were to be included in the borough of Merthyr, were thus purely mining villages, like villages in the Rhondda and elsewhere. Up in Merthyr itself, in Dowlais and Penydarren, coal continued to be mined primarily for the foundries. This did not prevent the ironmasters from going into the coal business; the Guest company – at that time Dowlais Ironworks – owned large pits down the valley and was responsible for one million of the two million tons mined in the entire Merthyr area in 1880. Also, since mining in the pick and shovel era required a vast amount of labour, there were always more men working below ground than above. Nevertheless, the character of Merthyr was that of an ironworking town rather than a mining town. This was its distinction in the South Wales industrial complex and its significance on the economic map of Britain.

In that Victorian high noon, another major change was on the way. From being an iron town, Merthyr was to become a steel town. Henry Bessemer, a brilliant engineer, had developed a revolutionary new process for steel-making. It was derided by many industrialists, but the Guest of that period saw its value, invited Bessemer to perfect his research at Dowlais, and adopted the method. The first Bessemer steel rails were produced at Dowlais in 1854. It was soon clear that Bessemer steel could be made far more quickly and more cheaply than any other steel, and Guest profited accordingly. The Crawshays, keeping up with the Guests as usual, converted Cyfarthfa into a steelworks a few years later.

Steel was to the later nineteenth century, and indeed the twentieth century, what iron had been to an earlier age – the dominant material in machine-making, in shipbuilding, and in countless branches of industry. Its particular importance for Merthyr was in the railway boom, which had now spread from Europe to the world. Lines thousands of miles long were being laid from New York to San Francisco, from Bombay to Delhi, from Moscow to Vladivostok. The rails had to be made in steel towns, and a good many of them were made in Merthyr.

Thus, over a long period of about a hundred and fifty years, the prosperity of Merthyr followed the graph of Britain's economic expansion. There were three peaks, which were also the peaks of British capitalism as measured by production, profits and employment. The first was the period of early industrialization, which saw the foundation of entire new industries and the mushroom growth of villages into great towns, and which was also stimulated by the effort of the Napoleonic wars. The second was what I have called the Victorian high noon, the proud years between 1850 and 1870, when Dickens created Mr Podsnap as a spokesman for British complacency and contempt for foreigners. A third peak was to come in the Edwardian golden twilight, when life for the middle classes was comfortable as never before, when Wells created Mr Ramage and Forster created Mr Wilcox.

Throughout this epoch, and especially when the peaks were reached, the accepted creed was that progress for industry and for 'the nation' meant progress for the workers too. Taking the long view, it was true; the wage-earning home had a carpet and an upright piano in the third peak, perhaps in the second peak, while in the first peak it certainly hadn't. But the long view misses a great deal that matters. It misses the deep valleys between the peaks – the prolonged depressions that endured (for instance) from 1815 to about 1835 after the war boom collapsed, and again intermittently from 1870 to 1900. And it omits a whole history of endurance and struggle while the extra shillings were being slowly wrested from the prior claims of profit. Seldom in the human record, and never under capitalism, has the history of those who work been quite the same as the history of those who possess.

4

One day in 1831, a crowd of working men in Merthyr Tydfil attacked and destroyed a building called Coffin's Court. Coffin was the name of a bailiff, and his business was to seize the property of debtors, or of people who were behind with the rent, and offer it for public auction. Property, one assumes, can have been nothing but a bed and a few chairs. Rashly, Coffin had just seized that of a man who was popular in the town and emerged as a leader in the events of the next few days. For the crowd went on to ransack the houses of about a hundred of 'the better class of citizens'. The rest of the 'better class', among them employers like Crawshay and Homfray, took refuge in the Castle Inn (where the Castle cinema is now). They sent a messenger for troops, and a force of Highlanders arrived. In a hand-to-hand struggle in the High Street, the soldiers were driven back into the inn; they then opened fire from the balcony. However, the people in the street had got hold of some of the Highlanders' muskets, to which they added home-made pikes and other weapons. Crawshay and his friends escaped to the Homfray residence, Penydarren House. For three days, the town was in the hands of its working people. All work in the mines and foundries stopped. The workers formed themselves into a kind of guerrilla army and put three military relief expeditions to flight. Ultimately, it took a thousand troops to restore order. Later, a man named Dic Penderyn was hanged after being convicted – falsely, it is practically certain – of having seized a bayonet and wounded a soldier in the thigh. On the day of his execution, industrial Wales showed its outrage in a widespread stoppage of work. In Merthyr, the name of

Dic Penderyn – a martyr to the panic and fury of the ruling classes – has never been forgotten.

Curiously, however, the Merthyr rising of 1831 has not become famous in the same way as the massacre of Peterloo, which after all was only a military onslaught on a peaceful crowd. What happened in Merthyr was (since Britain hasn't a history like that of France) the most serious rebellion in the last couple of centuries. It was far more than a riot; it was a seizure of power, if on a local scale; the rebels, though they soon dissipated their strength through disunity on aims and tactics, showed considerable skill in combat and immense courage. They deserved better than oblivion, and what they deserved they have at last received through the recent publication of Alexander Cordell's magnificent historical novel, *The Fire People*.

As well as telling the story of the rising and of Dic Penderyn, Cordell gives a detailed picture of working and living conditions in the Merthyr of the time. Those conditions were terrible to a degree that constitutes a lasting shame. True, the rising came in a year when the 'state of trade' was bad, unemployment was widespread, and the employers had cut wages by twenty per cent. But the known facts raise the larger question of whether the industrial revolution – for two or three generations, in Merthyr at least – was anything but a human disaster. Were the British people better off in the middle of the eighteenth century, when they lived in the countryside and worked on the land or in handicraft industry, or in the early nineteenth century when they lived in towns and worked in mills and factories?

This is a matter of keen controversy among historians – a controversy in which I am not qualified to join. Still, one thing appears certain. The period at which working people *felt* themselves to be better off – felt that life consisted of more than a struggle for survival – did not come until about 1850. By then, the great fortunes had been made, the Cyfarthfa Castles built; business was at last turning in the direction of supplying consumer goods, even to working people, and taking their purchasing power into account. Significantly, this marked the close of the age of unrest which we associate chiefly with the Chartist movement.

I am, perhaps, begging a question by speaking of 'working people'. The colliers and ironworkers of Merthyr were a working-class in the process of formation; they had been peasants, herded by blind economic forces into a new way of life, capable of rebellion and violence but with no collective strategy. They had no trade unions or political organizations of their own. When the besieged employers agreed to negotiate with a deputation from the thousands massed in the streets, this was in itself a huge turning-point. For, to men like William Crawshay, the rebels were not so much opponents as an instrument of production which had behaved unpredictably. He wrote afterwards: 'The fewness of the soldiers rendered the situation of the gentlemen in the Castle Inn extremely precarious; but the discipline and the valour of the Highlanders were beyond praise.' In fact, the Highlanders did not lose a man and the shots they fired at point-blank range from the balcony of the inn killed at least sixty men, women and children. This loss of life, Crawshay declared, was 'indeed dreadful'; but he consoled himself with the reflection that the dead were the guilty. And he pointed out further that the rebels showed their awareness of guilt by hiding the bodies and not producing the wounded for medical treatment. (At that time there was no hospital in Merthyr, though hospitals had been founded by philanthropic capitalists in many other towns.)

In Crawshay's unconscious revelation of the distinction he drew between the value of a gentleman's life and of a worker's, we are reminded of how an employer in a colonial country would see a riot on the plantation. The fact that he was English and men like Dic Penderyn were Welsh had something to do with it. If only because of the language barrier, the difference meant a great deal more than we can readily imagine.

Merthyr in the early nineteenth century, as several writers

have remarked, must have been more like a pioneer settlement on the American frontier – as we see it in Western films – than it was like an English town. The sudden flareup of violence, sparked by an individual injustice, shows that clearly enough. There was a district in the heart of the town, called China for some reason, rife with drinking-dens and brothels. The quantity of beer consumed in the town was prodigious, despite the efforts of the ministers. The mere handling of money, after life on the farm which was largely a matter of producing for one's own needs, was a transformation for the Wales of the time.

Money there certainly was. Figures given in 1815 show that a Lancashire weaver earned eight shillings a week; the average wage 'for workers of all classes' is reckoned (by G. D. H. Cole in *The Common People*) at eleven shillings during the war boom. Men in Merthyr were being paid a pound, or thereabouts. There seems no reason to doubt the conclusion of a historian who writes: 'The men who rose in arms in 1831 . . . frequently belonged, in terms of money wages, to the working-class élite of Britain'.

Against this, we have to set the psychological burden of relentless discipline and total dependence on the masters, for people whose fathers had at least ordered the routine of their own lives. We have to consider a working day of twelve hours, seven days a week. We have to think of the cruel toil of digging coal by hand or stoking furnaces, and the frequent accidents. Not least, we have to imagine the tiny hovels in which families lived, always close to the works and covered by smoke, without clean water or sanitation of any kind, in streets which the Health Commission, surveying Merthyr as late as 1845, called 'networks of filth, emitting noxious exhalations'. At that time more than half of the funerals in Merthyr were of children under the age of five.

This is not a detailed history, and it is sufficient to record that this situation – this disparity between a 'standard of living' measured in money terms, and the actual living experience of working people – continued into the twentieth century. To understand what it felt like, all this time, to live in Merthyr, four points must be made.

First, the industries made enormous profits and the owners enjoyed a way of life that was utterly remote from that of the workers – literally remote, indeed, after the Guests took themselves off to Wimborne in the pleasant Dorset countryside and the Crawshays to Caversham. Thanks to the nature of the industry, there were not many white-collar workers or 'staff' or workers with clean jobs: nothing like the complex society, with all its gradations of snobbery, that could be found in a city like London or even Cardiff. Class solidarity and class antagonism were facts that created themselves.

Secondly, wages in mining and in iron and steel continued to be above the working-class average. Piece-work was the rule, and men at the coal-face – if they wanted to use their muscles to the utmost – could reckon in boom times on earnings that would have made a clerk or a teacher jealous. In the years leading up to the First World War, there were cases (exceptional, but none the less real) of men in Merthyr earning £10 a week; at present-day prices this would be about £50, and no income tax. Wages like this, combined with the consciousness of doing 'a real man's job', made men content and indeed proud to spend a lifetime down the pit or at the foundry. They may have hated the bosses, but they didn't hate the industry.

Thirdly, however, wages were always dependent on 'the state of trade': on forces over which the workers had not a vestige of control. Big strikes during a period of general prosperity – in 1853, 1857, 1867 – were always against wage-cuts imposed by the employers because of a temporary drop in business. When a real recession came in the 1870s the Cyfarthfa works was closed and stayed closed for four years. In 1898, in another period of stagnation, the workers refused to accept a wage-cut and all the employers declared a lockout. After six months, poverty amounting almost to starvation compelled the workers to give in. Collective resistance through strong trade unions was manifestly the only safeguard for the miner and the steelworker.

Fourthly, social conditions in every sense continued to appal the humanitarian. Whatever figures were collected – living-space per head, infantile and maternal mortality, incidence of tuberculosis and other infectious diseases – they were invariably about the worst in the United Kingdom. Merthyr as a community could do little about all this, for the power and the money were always somewhere else. This is the reality behind Merthyr's long battle for borough status.

These factors shaped the political life of Merthyr, and indeed of South Wales. The first Reform Act entitled Merthyr to elect an MP, though on a franchise – there were 900 voters – limited to the 'better class'. Under the Second Reform Act, passed in 1867, Merthyr was combined with Aberdare, in the next valley to the west, to return two members; the system was that each elector had two votes, and there were normally three candidates. This Act gave the franchise to over 14,000 men, most of whom were working-class. Since 1918, Merthyr has been separated from Aberdare and has returned one member.

Merthyr has never had a trace of the working-class Toryism which has been since Disraeli's time, and still is, a considerable element in the politics of the Midlands or Lancashire. It was not the custom, until recent times, for parties to contest hopeless seats; and the appearance of a Conservative candidate in 1892 was an isolated event. He got 2,000 votes against 11,000 for each of the Liberals. In 1970 the Conservative saved his deposit by a bare margin, polling 3,169.

During the nineteenth century, and starting with Sir John Josiah Guest, no candidate stood a chance unless he announced himself as some kind of Liberal or radical. Some, to be sure, were more radical and indeed more liberal than others. But the working-class vote soon showed itself to be a force, apt to erupt as unpredictably as the rioters of 1831, if more peacefully. In 1868, with the workers enfranchised for the first time, they turned out the sitting member although he was a friend of Gladstone and had been a Liberal cabinet minister, to elect the radical Henry Richard. It is worth remarking that Richard never occupied himself much with 'bread and butter' grievances; he devoted his life to campaigning against war and militarism and for international arbitration. But he was enormously popular in Merthyr and held his seat easily until he died.

Merthyr belongs in Labour history as one of the first constituencies (though not the very first) to elect an avowed Socialist. The fact is, however, that the eclipse of Liberalism was a slow process. Keir Hardie, standing for the Independent Labour Party, came second in each of the four elections which he contested, being returned as 'junior member' for the double-member seat. He was always on friendly terms with the 'senior member', D. A. Thomas (later Lord Rhondda) although Thomas was a big local employer; what brought them together originally was opposition to the Boer War. A Liberal won Merthyr in 1918, and the ILP made it a stronghold only in 1922.

In modern times, it is generally assumed that the only contest that matters in Merthyr is for the Labour nomination. The 1935 election produced this remarkable result: Labour, 20,530; ILP, 9,640, no other candidate. The Council chamber has seen an occasional Communist or Welsh Nationalist or even 'Ratepayer', but the Labour majority is always overwhelming.

All the same, Merthyr still likes to do the unpredictable. In the run-up to the 1970 election, the Trades and Labour Council (as the local Politbureau is called) decided that the time had come for the sitting MP, S. O. Davies, to retire. Mr Davies had been in Parliament since 1934 and by the time of the election he was eighty-three years old – indeed, I've met people who assert that he was really eighty-six. However, he felt that he was still in full possession of his powers and insisted on standing again. This made him an independent candidate in opposition to the official Labour nominee, Mr Tal Lloyd. To the amazement and amusement of television commentators, Mr Davies won the election with almost a two-to-one majority.

Mr Davies died in February 1972. The man to be pitied in the by-election, as ever, is the Tory candidate – especially with unemployment at its present level.

5

'The workshop of the world' was no hollow phrase. The industrial supremacy enjoyed by Britain in the middle of the nineteenth century was unique in history; there had never been anything like it before, and it's highly unlikely that there ever will be again. For the nearest comparison we can recall a year like 1945, when Europe and the Soviet Union were crippled by war and Japan had not begun to count in the sphere of heavy industry. Clearly, the dominant industrial power was the United States; yet the American share of the world's output of manufactured goods was less than a half. Today there are several giants, each an impressive workshop but none entitled to call itself *the* workshop of the world.

But, in the mighty years whose symbol was the Great Exhibition of 1851, Britain produced something like three-quarters of all the goods in the world. In some major lines of production – locomotives and rolling-stock, heavy machinery, shipbuilding – there was practically a British monopoly. Less fortunate nations had to buy at the prices which Britain chose to fix and sell their raw materials for what Britain would pay. British overlords, responsible only to 'head office' in London, gave the orders at factories, railway stations, mines, plantations and even shops all over the world: not merely across the millions of square miles painted red on the map, but in nominally independent states such as Russia, the Ottoman Empire, China, Spain, Italy and the republics of Latin America. On top of the profits from trade, a vast invisible income poured in from investment by British banks in countries – notably the USA – which were rapidly developing but were short of capital.

Out in the Wild West, men armed with British-made guns held up British-made trains and made off with money whose loss had ultimately to be chalked up in the City of London.

Very few people, admiring the inventions displayed in the Crystal Palace, can have reflected that this supremacy rested on insecure foundations or that it was doomed to pass away. Still less could they have entertained the idea that decline was inherent in the very nature of the supremacy. More than a century later, it is easy to see how this was so.

The uniqueness of the 'workshop of the world' situation reveals, in hindsight, that it was a historical accident. Other nations were bound to follow the road that Britain had charted. If they were big nations, they were bound to catch up. The patriotic Englishman of the closing years of the century might wave his Union Jack as proudly as his father a generation before; but he could not deny that Britain had slipped to third place among steel-producing nations, behind the United States and Germany. He had heard of Edison lamps, Bell telephones, Diesel engines, and perhaps Benz motor-cars.

Also, just because Britain had been first in the field – in almost every field – her productive methods and her industrial equipment were bound to get out of date. Proud tradition attached to a cotton mill built in 1810, a pit sunk in 1840, a steelworks that had kept its furnaces alight since 1850; and, considering the investment that it represented, the Board of Directors was seldom inclined to scrap it and start again. But its foreign competitor, almost inevitably, was better designed and more efficient. Add to this that the bias in British industry, rooted in the habits of the early industrial revolution, was toward the clever mechanic in his shirt-sleeves rather than the scientist in his white coat. Once, these men in shirt-sleeves had done wonders in devising new methods and inventing new machines; later, they were busier in keeping machines going that ought to have been replaced. Apparent supremacy tempted British industry to roll along without the aids that became increasingly necessary – research and advanced technical education. While British universities turned out clergymen, lawyers and recruits for the Indian Civil Service, German universities were training chemists and physicists whose work was to revolutionize many branches of production and make entire factories into useless museum-pieces.

Then, if American industry as we know it today is not the 'workshop of the world', that is in part because its output is largely directed toward a home market of two hundred million people. The 'workshop of the world' conception itself indicates that nineteenth-century Britain was producing to a great extent for export, and relied on export for its profits. Britain created the overseas markets, and for a time Britain dominated them because she made the goods – the only goods. Sooner or later, the customers were bound to start making the goods for themselves. They did: first the developing industrial nations like America, France and Germany; then less powerful countries like Italy: finally even subjects of the Queen (by 1900 there was a growing Indian textile industry, owned by Indians). Sooner or later, too – though British influence was able to maintain the system of world free trade for a surprising length of time – other nations were likely to protect their industries by tariffs raising the prices of British goods. Meanwhile, as foreign industries reached maturity and were able to export, the traditional markets were no longer a British preserve. Faced by competition, British exporters had to cut their profit margins. Even so, foreign products made by more modern methods began to capture the markets.

By the turn of the century, all these changes were far advanced. Britain remained complacent; and a major reason was that British investment abroad, and the export of British capital, remained at a high level and even increased. In that Edwardian golden twilight, the dividends and the wealth of the great banks were more satisfying than ever. But what Britain now enjoyed was a financial supremacy, not a true industrial supremacy as in the past. Britain, in fact, was living on her fat. In 1913, the United States was still marginally a debtor nation – the debts being to Britain as they had been for decades. A few years later, Britain was asking for American loans to finance the war effort.

Finally, there was one question too disturbing to be asked. The health of world capitalism, and in particular Britain's ability to remain rich despite a worsening relative position, depended on unchecked progress and continuous expansion. Words like 'unchecked' and 'continuous' could never be taken literally; there were recurrent crises and depressions, with distinctly unpleasant effects. Still, the general trend was onward and upward. What would happen in the event of a real upset? A devastating world war: a red revolution taking a major nation out of the whole system and spreading anxiety in others: a cut-throat tariff battle; a slump on a scale yet unknown, with a world-wide decline in production – something like that? No one knew how to cope with any of these calamities. Starting in 1914, all four of them happened.

In every respect that I have described, no spot on the industrial map of Britain was more vulnerable than Merthyr Tydfil. First in the field every time, its industries had been getting steadily more ancient. Even the steelworks, the most recent development, dated from the 1850s and used processes that would have caused (and probably did cause) smiles at Essen and Gary, Indiana. Where a centre like Birmingham could call itself 'a city of a thousand trades', Merthyr – and indeed South Wales – had all its eggs in one or at most two baskets; it produced nothing but coal and steel, and employed men untrained to do anything else. These products were the materials of industry, or the fuel for industry, and not goods to be sold to consumers, so that any jolt in the economy as a whole was sure to react on Merthyr. Last but not least, the export trade was absolutely essential to the way that Merthyr functioned.

Already, right in the heyday of British supremacy, there had been a warning of what could happen to Merthyr. Iron, once the foundation of the town's growth, became an obsolete industry. The Penydarren works closed down in 1859, the Plymouth works in 1880. True, the wounds were healed because the Dowlais and Cyfarthfa works, which in any case were the largest, went over to steel – Penydarren and Plymouth lacked the capital to do so. But this redoubled the concentration of ownership which had been so marked all along. Two companies now owned the only industrial undertakings in the town itself; and it will be recalled that one of them, the Guest concern, also owned many of the mines in the other villages belonging to the borough. Never since the eighteenth century had the fortunes of Merthyr been so heavily dependent on the Guests and the Crawshays.

Then came another warning. Changes in the technique of steel-making meant that it became advisable to use imported iron-ore, chiefly from Spain, instead of the Welsh variety. This in turn meant that the best place for a steelworks was at a port, not up in the mountains; and in 1889 the Guests opened a new works in Cardiff. Business was prosperous enough to keep the old Dowlais works going too, but it was easy to guess which the directors would maintain if they ever had to make a choice. As for the Cyfarthfa works, the cost of bringing Spanish ore up the railway made it a lame duck. After struggling on for a while, it closed down in 1910. The workers either found jobs at Dowlais or went into the pits, which fortunately were producing flat out at the time. Cyfarthfa was put into production again during the 1914-18 war, but closed for ever in 1920.

The year 1913 can be taken as the high-point for Merthyr. The population stood at 84,000, comfortably above the qualifying figure for borough status. Indeed, Merthyr had been a county borough and administratively independent of Glamorgan for eight years; the Council had bought Cyfarthfa Castle and was planning all kinds of improvements. Unemployment – figures were being recorded for the first time, because Lloyd George had brought in a system of unemployment insurance – was a negligible 1.4%. The pits in the borough area produced just over three million tons of coal, and the attainment of this magic figure caused a great deal of local pride. The coal figures for South Wales as a whole (both production and export) were a record too. Only malcontents pointed to another kind of record for 1913 – in the number of deaths in mining accidents.

But, as a background to what happened later, it is worth looking at the pattern of employment. The danger signal is clear enough to the eye of hindsight: the overwhelming concentration of jobs in the basic industries of steel and coal, and of ownership – which means control of employment – in the hands of a few big firms, primarily the Guest company. To begin with, there were practically no jobs for women except for about 900 in domestic service (a remarkable number considering the scantiness of Merthyr's middle-class). The lack of women's jobs in industry, by contrast with a textile or cigarette-making town, meant that the number of dependants for each male worker was perilously large. For the men, there were 32,000 jobs in the borough: 24,000 for miners, 3,500 for steelworkers (a reduced number since Cyfarthfa had closed), and 4,500 others. Among these 4,500 we have to reckon all the railwaymen and bus-drivers, building workers and dustmen, gas and electricity employees, clerks and municipal officials, shopkeepers, teachers, ministers of religion (over 100 of these) and whatever else you can think of.

That was Merthyr, on the edge of catastrophe.

6

The end of the First World War was followed by a hectic boom, with factories working round the clock to turn out the goods which had vanished from the shops in wartime. Wages went up rapidly, although prices went up too and not many working-class families were better off. The boom was patchy as well as hectic and visible mainly in consumer goods and services; basic industries such as coal and steel contracted from their wartime activity, and it was in a boom year that the Cyfarthfa steelworks was finally closed. Miners found, for the first time, that their wages were below instead of above the working-class average. At the end of 1920, barely two years after the Armistice, the boom abruptly collapsed. By March 1921 there were 1,500,000 unemployed, more than in any previous spell of hard times. By the end of the year, the figure was almost two million.

Suddenly, coal was an ailing industry. Modern ships were running on oil, and factories in countries without coal resources were tending to use either oil or hydro-electric power; these changes had been in evidence for some time, but had been masked before the war by the general expansion. Foreign countries had learned in wartime to do without British coal, and a market once lost is not easily recovered. German and Polish mines were selling at prices which Britain could not meet. It became clear that the export trade would never regain anything like the peak of 1913, and the drop in home sales when the boom collapsed made matters worse. In 1921 the mine-owners confessed that their books wouldn't balance, and a Royal Commission recommended the nationalisation of the industry. The Government rejected this advice; as for the owners, they preferred the time-honoured remedy of cutting wages. The miners fought back by going on strike. They were defeated, and when the pits opened again more foreign markets had disappeared. The Government now stepped in and gave the industry a subsidy, but this solution was obviously temporary.

By the end of 1921 there were 16,000 miners at work in Merthyr instead of 24,000. The small and old-fashioned pits up in the mountains were the first to be hit; independent owners went bankrupt, so the big companies bought the pits and shut them down in the name of 'rationalisation'. However, there were also closures and lay-offs (the word 'redundancy' hadn't been invented) among the deep pits in the Taf valley. Of the 8,000 miners who lost their jobs, a few found other work, some were at or near retirement age, and some – the first wave of a migration – left Wales to see if things were more hopeful in other parts of Britain. The great majority had to live on the dole. But the unemployment figures convey less than the full truth about the disaster that had struck Merthyr, for the miners who still had jobs were generally working only three or four days a week. As they were paid by the shift, or by piece-work for the tonnage they produced, their earnings were sharply reduced. After all their proud history, the mining valleys were a place of poverty.

The next few years brought a partial respite, mainly because German coal production was halted during the French occupation of the Ruhr. But by 1925 things were bad again, and the Government's insistence on returning to the gold standard, together with the onset of a fierce tariff war, priced British exports decisively out of the market. Next year, this Conservative Government – with Stanley Baldwin as Prime Minister and Winston Churchill, whose memory is less revered in Merthyr than in Epping, as Chancellor of the Exchequer – ended the coal subsidy. The mine-owners declared the wage-cuts must come into force at once. The General Strike, called in support of the miners, ended in defeat after nine days; the miners' strike continued for nine grim months and ended in defeat too.

Though world capitalism was considered to be in good health again by the later 1920s, unemployment in Britain never melted away; it was to stay above the one million mark from war to war. The really bad times began in 1929. A day of panic in Wall Street put paid to the dreams of a 'plateau of stability' and as the economic crisis spread throughout the capitalist world, to the accompaniment of spectacular bank failures and industrial bankruptcies, experts plotted the graphs of a depression whose like had never been seen before. There were several graphs: production and international trade going down, unemployment going up in the United States, in Germany (where the result was Hitler) and not least in Britain. In September 1931, the month of the political crisis that led to the formation of a 'national' Government, the total was nearly three million. It did not fall to any real extent until late in 1933.

Throughout the 'thirties, unemployment was a curse that could not be exorcised. But it was not evenly spread throughout industry or throughout the country. Where there was a range of light industry and a boom (aided by low mortgage rates) in private house-building, it was just possible to believe the current saloon-bar wisdom that 'there's plenty of work for those who want it.' The mass unemployment in the true sense of the term was in the old-established basic industries, the veterans of British capitalism. In 1936, a year when partial recovery had halved the peak national total, unemployment was still at 25% in the mining industry. That industry was third in a list of 35 'occupations' hit by unemployment, with only public works contracting and shipbuilding showing a worse percentage. And within the mining industry, South Wales with its many obsolete pits was putting more men on the dole than a more modern coalfield such as Nottinghamshire. Coal production in South Wales had declined from 54 million tons in 1923 (a far from brilliant year) to 35 million in 1935. Moreover, men were being thrown out of work by a gradual turn to new methods; during the same period, the percentage of Welsh coal cut by machine rose from 4% to 18%.

The regional figures for 1936 are the most revealing. Unemployment was 6.5% in London and only 5.6% in the South-east; in Scotland it was 18% and in Wales, the worst hit region of all, 28.5%. These figures illustrate another fact: neither the coal industry nor Wales shared in the recovery, such as it was. An investigation by a Labour Party team elicited the fact that, in industrial Wales, over half of the men on the dole had been on it for more than a year – one in eight of them for more than five years. In Merthyr, 1934 was reckoned to be the worst year of the slump. No real hope appeared on the horizon until the Second World War.

And, where the mines were the principal source of a livelihood, unemployment was still only one side of the coin of poverty, low wages being the other. In a table of male workers' earnings for 1931, coal stands twentieth in the list of twenty-two industries, just above cotton and agriculture. The average printing worker was getting £3.55 (using the decimal system), the building worker £2.81, the miner £2.30 – provided that he worked five shifts in the week, which was the exception and not the rule. Of course, prices were low. But if we multiply these earnings by four, which is the right adjustment for the present value of money, they are still the earnings of poverty.

In that table, the steel industry ranks about midway with average earnings of £2.74. The worst blow that struck Merthyr in the depression was that there was no longer a steel industry. In 1930 the Dowlais steelworks was closed and 3,400 jobs disappeared overnight. All that remained was a small plant belonging to Guest, Keen & Nettlefold, making ingot moulds and at present employing 500 workers. From the 'slip road' which runs from Pentrebach to Dowlais, one can still gaze at the remnants of the steelworks – a huge concrete foundry-casing lying on its side, cuttings where rails once ran and now there's only grass, an iron footbridge leading from nowhere to nowhere, a single tall brick chimney waiting for a storm violent enough to topple it. The foundations of the main building, in great blocks of stone, are indestructible and one can trace the dimensions from them, as one might trace the dimensions of a medieval castle or of Solomon's temple. That is all – that, and the White Tip.

The closing of the Dowlais works, which ended Merthyr's long history as an iron and steel town, is well remembered as the classic instance of how human lives were left to the mercy of economic forces. I talked to an old man who worked up to the last day as a skilled machine-fitter; ironically, he is now the night-watchman for the contractors who are removing the White Tip. They'll find some strange things in that tip, he says. Once, a locomotive plunged over the cliff with its load; once, a fire-engine drawn by four horses. Dowlais was known as Pegleg Town because there were so many accidents. But, he insists, it was the finest steelworks in the world. Nothing was turned out but the very best. He remembers working day and night for a week to build a loading-bank for rails a hundred feet long. They were never made – Krupp's got the contract, he thinks. He talks with that curious Merthyr combination of pride in the industry and contempt for the company. Curious, yet logical: it was the company that gave up, not the workers. King Edward, looking at Dowlais in 1936, made the right point. 'Something must be done for these people,' he said, 'after all, they were brought here for this works'.

The Dowlais shut-down had several consequences. It took away the one industrial enterprise that kept going all through the week and paid anything like decent wages. It caused the final extinction of the collieries in the mountain area, which had always been ancillary to iron and steel-making. Thus, it made the town of Merthyr into a place with practically no industrial work whatever. Since hardly anyone had any money to spend beyond the bare necessities, this drastically affected such other work as there was. People no longer employed painters or plumbers. Small street-corner shops ceased to exist. Half the pubs – that is, of those counted in 1921 – were closed. Widows who had lived by taking in washing or having single men as lodgers could no longer do so. They had not been insured workers, so they were not listed among the unemployed; but they had been earning their keep, and now they had to apply for relief.

In 1934, there were only 8,000 miners employed in Merthyr. In other words, out of every three jobs in the pits available in 1913, one had gone by 1921 and another one in the depression. There were still jobs in the deep pits of the valley and there were some jobs right away from Merthyr; 1,000 people were travelling anything up to 24 miles to work. The count of unemployed was 12,460, or 63.6% of insured workers. This has to be seen as an average, because the borough includes the villages where pits were never closed. The Employment Exchange had, and still has, three sub-offices tabulating their own figures – in the town of Merthyr, at Dowlais, and at Treharris to cover the valley communities. In that year of 1934, unemployment in Dowlais was 80%. I have met a man – now a well-paid technician – who recalls that when he was at school, only two out of the forty-five children in the class had fathers who were earning. One was the son of the vicar, the other was the son of a policeman.

The dole, or unemployment benefit, was then £1.36 for a man with a wife and two children. A single man was supposed to manage on 76p, a single woman on 67½p. Since the scheme was based on contributions made when in work, benefit as a right ran out after twenty-six weeks. Thereafter, the unemployed were dependent on Public Assistance. The scales were about the same, but the payment could be reduced by the operation of the means test – a stringent inquiry into any other sources of income, such as casual handicraft work, and the earnings of other members of the family even if they were not living at home or in fact giving any help. A local authority could grant a small amount of relief on its own account – this was a relic of the old 'parish relief' system – and Merthyr was more generous than some far more wealthy communities. After all, some of the councillors were on the dole. Still, the man who had the biggest influence on the standard of living was the Public Assistance officer responsible to the Government. The flavour of the 'thirties can be recaptured by quoting a regulation made by this officer in Merthyr:

'No applications in respect of rent, clothing, coal, etc. to be entertained, but boots may be granted to men who have been unemployed for twelve months or more if they obtain regular employment. The first day's earnings of Sandwich-Board Carriers may be ignored; no relief to be granted to Rag and Bone Gatherers'.

During these years, quite a lot of calculations were made by nutritional experts to work out the minimum sum on which a family could maintain life and health, and it always added up to more than the unemployed were getting. I don't propose to quote these calculations – merely to say that, as in the distant days of the industrial revolution, the population of Merthyr were struggling for existence. Life can be maintained, somehow or other, on a level below what experts think possible. As for health, in most cases it simply wasn't maintained.

I am old enough to remember driving through Merthyr in the 'thirties – there was no Heads of the Valleys Road then – on the way to holidays on the Gower coast. There were always more men in the High Street than women: men chatting, or passing a newspaper from hand to hand, or staring into shop windows, or doing nothing. In London, I remember groups singing in the streets with a placard that said 'Welsh Miners'. My father liked me to put a few coppers in the cloth cap on the pavement, because we were Welsh. These are unforgettable memories; but of course, they are marginal to my life. On that march to Cyfarthfa Park, I was walking with men and women who lived through it all.

7

In 1934, as I have said, there were over 12,000 unemployed in Merthyr. In 1939, there were only 7,000. One might draw the deduction that 5,000 jobs had been made available. If so, one would be wrong.

When the depression came, the Welsh mining valleys – along with Tyneside and similar regions – were given the officialese name of Distressed Areas. In 1936, as Britain was supposed to be recovering, they were more euphemistically renamed Special Areas. Among expert advisers and civil servants, two schools of thought arose, and it is important to summarize their views because both are still with us.

The assumption on which they agreed was that places like Merthyr could never regain full employment on the basis of coal and steel. One school took the view that Merthyr was a hopeless case and its decline was inevitable. The other believed that a rescue was possible through the introduction of new industries.

Naturally enough, the latter view was the one voiced in public by Government spokesmen. In 1936, the Special Areas Reconstruction Act was passed as a planning framework for the rescue operation. The trouble was that the Government then possessed very few techniques of the 'carrot' variety, and none at all of the 'stick' variety, to get the new industries where they were needed. Moreover, the economy as a whole was still far from booming. In the end, it was the war and only the war that ended the depression. In 'our finest hour', when the Army fought its way home from Dunkirk, the Britain that stood alone against Hitler still had one million unemployed, a fact that remains the most eloquent condemnation of how its affairs had been managed between the wars.

In the last couple of years of peace, new industries did begin to trickle into Merthyr: a branch factory of Imperial Chemical Industries, a Rotax engineering works, a firm making stockings and another firm making buttons. Altogether, they provided 900 jobs.

How, then, did the numbers of the unemployed diminish? Some Merthyr people found jobs in new 'trading estates', where modern factories had arrived with official encouragement, at Treforest, eighteen miles down the road to Cardiff, and at Hirwaun, eight miles to the west. But they were far outnumbered by those who left Merthyr altogether.

Welshmen, in fact, were voting with their feet against the hopelessness that surrounded them. Those who were qualified scattered themselves across England as white-collar workers in modern offices, doctors, or teachers. The rest took whatever jobs they could find in areas where unemployment was light. Being in effect immigrants, they mostly got unskilled jobs; they dug ditches, emptied rubbish-bins, worked on building sites, or washed up dishes in hotels, while the girls became housemaids in an age when the word 'au pair' was still unknown. The lucky ones got into factories; Slough, whose trading estate was about the most successful of the 'thirties, still has a sizeable Welsh population. The most unlucky never found jobs and went on singing in the streets. Some Welshmen emigrated in the full sense to Australia, South Africa, Canada; some joined the armed forces.

In the depression years up to 1935, according to the Labour Party investigation which I have mentioned, 292,000 people left industrial Wales (the counties of Glamorgan and Monmouth). Since no passports were shown, the exact figures are a matter for argument, but the total must in any case have been something like a tenth of the population. Roughly, this meant a fifth of the young men – a deprivation comparable to that caused by a devastating war. Girls had difficulty in finding husbands, and the population acquired an imbalance which remains to this day. In Merthyr, the exodus was greater than in most other communities. The borough's population fell, from its 1913 peak of 84,000, to a 1939 figure of 61,000.

There was a similar movement from all the old strongholds of the industrial revolution – Scotland, Lancashire, Tyneside. As G. D. H. Cole wrote: 'This made the Britain of 1938 a good deal more like the Britain of 1746 than it was like, say, the Britain of 1850.' It was the start, indeed, of the drift to the south-east that has worried planners ever since. Despite the low birth-rate of the period, the population of London and the Home Counties went up by 14%. People who lived there began complaining about suburban sprawl, loss of open country, traffic congestion and the other problems which they complain about now.

In Merthyr and similar places, the effects were bad in a different way and the complaints were more bitter. People, for the most part, loved their homes and migrated only from harsh necessity. Those who stayed behind saw their towns and villages becoming derelict communities. The first to leave, naturally, were the young, the intelligent and the ambitious whose talents could have helped Merthyr to recover. As a percentage of the population, non-productive groups who had to be 'carried' by the community bulked larger and larger: that is, young children, pensioners, the ageing unemployed who had little hope of working again, and the victims of mining accidents or coal-dust in the lungs. By the mid-thirties, Merthyr as a borough was literally insolvent.

In 1935, the Government appointed a Royal Commission to report on whether Merthyr should keep its hard-won status as a county borough. The evidence presented a gloomy picture of a declining town; a witness from Dowlais, for instance, said that he was living among 'hundreds of vacant houses'. The rates had trebled during the depression years and were the highest in Britain, but their yield was the lowest of any authority of similar size. All the basic services were running at a deficit. As the Commission saw things, the Council had been culpably living beyond its means, especially in the provision of relief and in its standards of education; Merthyr was proud of its schools and had 22% of the young people going on to secondary education, an exceptional percentage in the Britain of the time. On the Gradgrind principles by which the Commission worked, the case for taking away borough status was irrefutable. Thanks to the emigration, Merthyr no longer had even the requisite population, let alone the requisite financial resources. The Mayor and other citizens put up a determined fight, declaring stoutly that their relief scales were a human necessity and good schools were an investment in a better future. The county of Glamorgan told the Commission that it had not the least desire to take on responsibility for Merthyr. Nevertheless, the Commission recommended that the county borough should be abolished. As it happened, nothing was done and it was left to the Redcliffe-Maud commission on local government to make just the same recommendation in 1969. (The present Government's decision is that Merthyr should be a district in the new county of Mid-Glamorgan, which will separate the valleys from Cardiff and Swansea.)

Reading the Commission's bloodless prose today, one can clearly discern the thinking that dismissed Merthyr as a hopeless case – 'a dying town', as the phrase went. But that phrase bears scrutiny. Towns do not die of their own accord, or through ailments that can't be helped, or from diseases impossible to diagnose, as individuals sometimes do. Even men and women, come to that, die quite often from diseases caused by wretched housing or evil conditions of work, from causes that are a social responsibility and a social shame – and that was emphatically true in what officialdom itself called the Distressed Areas. For the sickness of a town, for mass unemployment and emigration, one has to find the causes in deliberate decisions: decisions such as the closing of the Dowlais steelworks, or at the other end of Britain the closing of the Jarrow shipyards. That the decisions were made by men who had no option within the limits of the economic system is simply an indictment of the system – of blind forces operating ruthlessly at the expense of human dignity and happiness. Ellen Wilkinson wrote a book about Jarrow and called it *The Town That Was Murdered*. A book about Merthyr could have had no truer title.

Before war came, Merthyr received the attention of one more investigating committee, not Government-appointed this time, but set up by an organisation that commanded much respect in educated, including liberal and progressive, quarters. In 1939, Political and Economic Planning published a report that took the 'hopeless case' school of thought to its logical conclusion. It pointed out that, in one way and another, each inhabitant of Merthyr was costing the British taxpayer £1 a week. This subsidy merely enabled Merthyr people to live at subsistence level in what PEP described as 'one of the least habitable districts of England and Wales'. Surely they couldn't want to go on living there if they had any alternative. The right thing to do, PEP concluded, was to abandon Merthyr altogether and move all the people to a new town, either in the Vale of Usk or on the coast of Glamorgan.

It wasn't the kind of thing that the Government of 1939, whose indifference to 'dying towns' exceeded any actual ill-will, could ever have found the energy or the money to do. But it showed what enlightened people, and experts in planning, drawn mainly from the leading universities, considered wise and even humane. Planning itself was then a novelty; the idea that planning should aim at enabling people to live according to their own aspirations, rather than at designing a scheme that pleased the planners, had yet to occur to such experts. Nor was it really accepted even after the 'bad old days' were supposedly relegated to an irrelevant past. In 1952, with Merthyr as close as it has ever come to full recovery, a PhD thesis by a Mr Belshaw of Selwyn College, Cambridge, concluded that the PEP scheme would have been 'the best solution'. He described it, indeed, as 'a novel and important experiment, which would have been specially interesting to the geographer'. The title-page of the thesis doesn't tell us what is Mr Belshaw's field of study, but I imagine that he is a geographer.

So in 1939, with the German Army massing on the Polish frontier and the Royal Air Force pleading for aircraft, the unemployed of Merthyr were still hanging about the streets or killing time in the public library, where they could read about PEP's final solution to their problems. They must have felt that Merthyr had reached rock-bottom.

8

Ernest Bevin had a story that he was fond of telling; when he was visiting an Army unit on the eve of D-Day, a soldier called out to him: 'Are we going back to the dole after this lot, Ernie?' If the soldier came from Merthyr, the question had a special point. For the men from Merthyr did go back to the dole, though mercifully not for long.

Certainly, the war ended the depression. The need for coal was acute; mining was a reserved occupation, and even young men who wanted to get into uniform found themselves directed to the pits, which is why there are only six names on Merthyr's war memorial plaque. Other work was available in war industry, notably in a big ordnance factory at Hirwaun. This engineering work introduced new skills and gave Merthyr confidence in a future with a new industrial basis. Moreover, out of the 5,600 new jobs created by the war, half were for women. This broke down traditional prejudices about woman's place being in the home, and provided many families with a double income.

Pessimists could point out that, even at the height of the war, the unemployment register did not entirely vanish. Elderly men in poor health, who could have been used in some capacity in a big city, stayed on the dole because the range of work in Merthyr was still limited. Also, the new opportunities were mostly not in Merthyr; if things became difficult again, people from Aberdare and elsewhere would be competing for Hirwaun jobs. But these were minor problems when set against the misery of pre-war days.

Then came victory: for Merthyr, a mixed blessing. Promptly in July 1945, the Hirwaun ordnance factory closed down. In 1946, there were 7,000 unemployed. A sizeable number of them were women who had become insured workers during the war; compared with 1939, when 7,000 unemployed meant 7,000 men out of work – each the mainstay of a family, if he was married – the situation was not so bad. It was, nevertheless, pretty rough. If it continued, the war would figure in Merthyr's history as a mere interlude in depression and decline.

It certainly would have continued if the blind economic forces had been allowed to operate without interference. Action to redirect those forces – action fiercely denounced by businessmen as red tape, ignorant meddling and a negation of freedom – was by far the greatest factor in bringing fresh work to Merthyr and to the other old unemployment black-spots. The Labour Government elected in 1945 was lucky in inheriting a structure of powerful controls devised for war purposes. It used these, and created others, to get factories built in places which employers would never have considered if in full possession of their 'freedom'.

There were both sticks and carrots. The carrots were investment grants, handed out to firms which provided work in the old Special Areas – now called Development Areas, with certain places (including Merthyr and the Welsh valleys) distinguished as Special Development Areas and carrying extra grants. Building grants, tax reliefs, cheap ground rents and low-interest loans also featured among the carrots. Left-wing critics declared that capitalists were waxing rich on these aids and were being bribed to do what was no more than their duty, but Labour Ministers took the view that this was inevitable in a mixed economy. There was no direction of industry, and the stick was in the nature of aversion therapy rather than positive command. It took the form of the Industrial Development Certificate, a permit which a firm had to obtain before it could put up a new factory. The IDC was granted seldom in a congested region like southeastern England, rather more generously in the average industrial district, and with a cheerful pat on the back only in a Development Area, where the firm aiming at expansion often ended up by process of elimination. The IDC system influenced not only new projects, but also plant which had been bombed in the war and could be rebuilt only in a place where it was needed in the Government's opinion.

Thanks to these inducements and controls, several new factories were built in Merthyr during the Attlee Government's six years of power. Much the most important was an imposing plant built by the Hoover company, principally making washing machines, at Pentrebach, a convenient location between the town and the valley villages. As it grew, this was to provide Merthyr with well over two thousand jobs (the actual payroll was even larger, but workers came in from as far afield as Caerphilly). Teddington Aircraft Controls moved in from its former home at Sunbury-on-Thames. Employing 1,500 workers at its peak, this was particularly welcome because it made highly sophisticated equipment for aircraft; it needed skilled engineers rather than assembly-line workers, and was willing to train them. Third in size was the Triang factory, making toy cars with that brand-name and Pedigree prams, and providing 800 jobs. All three firms came from outer London; Hoover's parent factory and head office are at Perivale, Triang's at Merton. In that environment, where factories are as thick on the ground as churches in Rome, they would presumably have expanded had they been free from control.

Others came too – Thorn Electrical (making light-bulbs), O.P. Chocolates, Kayser-Bondor Stockings, and a number of smaller firms each contributing its fifty or a hundred to the employment total. The coal shortage continued in peacetime for a dozen years, and the National Coal Board went all out to attract recruits with posters featuring a cheerful miner and the words: 'In the Mines – It's a Job for Life!' The Council started a major building programme, which has by now provided 5,000 houses or flats. In 1952, unemployment was down to 1,400. In good years during the 'fifties and 'sixties, it went below the thousand mark.

All this, certainly, was a tremendous change: from mass unemployment to almost full employment, and from dependence on basic industries owned by a couple of companies to a considerable diversity of work, most of it clean and relatively pleasant and a good deal of it skilled. Figures collected in 1969 sum up the transformation. Out of 23,000 insured workers – nearly 8,000 of them women – there were 9,000 employed in engineering and manufacturing, a total that amply made up for the jobs lost in steel. There was still, however, a clear difference between the town of Merthyr and the villages represented by the Department of Employment's Treharris office. In the latter, 2,300 out of 3,200 jobs were in the mines and only 418 women were at work.

In the greatly improved situation, there were still several snags. One was the 'almost' in 'almost full employment'. Merthyr, and indeed Wales, never quite caught up with the favoured parts of the country. The conditions that appeared in the South-east and the Midlands during the boom of the Macmillan years, with firms crying out for labour and paying above the established rates to lure workers from their rivals, remained alien to Merthyr's experience. You could never change your job at will; if you were at Hoover's or Teddington's, you tried to stay for ten or twenty years. If you lost your job, you expected at least a short spell on the dole. When unemployment nationally was one per cent (which means a labour shortage in Coventry) it was two per cent in Merthyr; when the national figure was two per cent, Merthyr's was four.

It had become clear over the years that 'stick and carrot' methods were not adequate to eliminate unemployment or to wipe out disparities between the regions. The IDC system gradually lost its effectiveness, partly because it was used less strictly by Conservative Governments, partly because there was a loophole: no IDC was needed to put machines into an existing building and, after the war losses were made good, a firm could usually find a building to buy from another firm closing down or moving. As for the carrots, they could be disregarded in periods when profits were easy anyway. A company might reckon that the saving in transport costs by being near the London market outweighed the grants given for being in Merthyr. By 1971, when unemployment was serious again, Wales presented this picture: non-Development Areas 3.9% unemployed, Development Areas 5.6%, Special Development Areas 6.4% – which, of course, was precisely the wrong way round.

With all the progress that had been made, there were never enough jobs in Merthyr for Merthyr's people. The figures I have cited show 4,000 of them – one worker out of six – working outside the quite extensive borough boundaries. Far more serious was the continuing emigration. Since the war, the population of Britain has risen by 20%, chiefly because of a rising birth-rate and major advances in health, such as the conquest of tuberculosis. These factors have been at work in Merthyr too, and yet its population has fallen by another 3,000 to a low point, at the present time, of 58,000. Emigration can be the only reason. Today as in the past, it is masking the full reality of unemployment.

What persisted in Merthyr was the sense of insecurity which had become second nature. It was felt that the products now being made there, such as washing-machines, depended on an unsteady market and on such factors as tighter or easier hire-purchase – and some, such as stockings or toy cars, simply on fashion. It was felt, also, that the companies didn't really belong to Merthyr and would pull out if the whim seized them or if they got into trouble. Most of them, in fact, did have larger factories elsewhere. If the Dowlais steelworks had gone after 170 years in Merthyr, it was argued, Hoover's might go after a mere twenty-five. Recently, one intelligent man told me that he'd heard on good authority that Hoover's wouldn't stay in Merthyr for a year after Britain entered the Common

c

Market. I have not a shred of evidence for this prophecy, and I quote it as an illustration of Merthyr insecurity. One consequence of this caution is that Merthyr people don't themselves start up small businesses, which would anyway be contrary to working-class tradition. Another is that they save their money and spend relatively little on ephemeral consumer goods or entertainment; thus, unintentionally, they limit the creation of new jobs in the service sector. Even when it was the fashion to talk about the 'affluent society', Merthyr was on the roadside watching.

You may say, as I heard an English voice say loudly in the lounge of the New Inn, that Merthyr ought to forget about the 'thirties and get rid of its complexes. But it isn't so simple. 'Once bitten, twice shy' is an enduring sentiment, and 'bitten' is a mild word for what Merthyr has suffered. And, just as Merthyr received some jolts in the heyday of Victorian prosperity, so it also took a few knocks in the buoyant 1960s.

To start with, the Coal Board's jolly posters turned into a bad joke when the experts decided – wrongly, as it has turned out – that coal was a drug on the market and oil or nuclear power would meet most of Britain's fuel needs. Pits deemed obsolete were closed down wholesale, and no region lost more of them than South Wales. Recruiting virtually stopped; redundancies or 'early retirements' ran into the thousands. Merthyr was affected less drastically than most other Welsh mining areas; only five pits are left out of more than a score, but they are big ones and (I hope) their future is secure. Still, out of those 32,000 jobs underground which existed in 1913 – of which there were still 8,000 in the depression – only 3,000 or so remain today.

Then, in 1964, the ICI plant was closed. Like Guest, Keen & Nettlefold in 1930, ICI decided that the coast of the Bristol Channel made a better location. This was a shock, for the plant had been in Merthyr since 1939 and its arrival was remembered as the first gleam of hope after the darkest years.

Another Labour Government was elected. Merthyr people, putting in their usual overwhelming vote, hoped for an era of economic growth – based on all that technology of which Harold Wilson spoke so glowingly – in which they would take what they saw as their rightful part. The growth never came; and in 1966, three months after another election which gave the Government a solid majority, it introduced a severe economic squeeze which soon put the national unemployment figures up to 500,000. There, or thereabouts, they stayed until they took a further upward bound under Edward Heath.

9

The departure of ICI had left a quite impressive stretch of land and empty buildings just alongside the Heads of the Valleys Road. Making a virtue of necessity, the Council declared this property to be an industrial estate and invited industrialists to set up their businesses there. No one could say that the inducements were niggardly. If a firm wanted to use the existing buildings, the Council would help to pay for any necessary adaptation; if it chose to build, the land was offered at a derisory rent of 5p a square yard. This, of course, was additional to the Government's investment grant. Despite these temptations, the estate is still only partly occupied, and the number of workers there – even if it's boosted by including employees of a printing works which moved from old premises elsewhere in Merthyr – has never reached the number formerly employed by ICI.

One firm which did come, however, was a foundry and engineering enterprise called Cold Precision Forgings. CPF is believed in Merthyr to have collected £500,000 from the Government as a reward for the move, taking one grant with another. The Council handed out £50,000 to have buildings adapted to suit its requirements. But in 1970, after five years in Merthyr, CPF decided to close down and dismiss its 140 workers, stating apologetically that its market research had been faulty. Then, having presumably done some fresh research, the company opened up again at Bromsgrove, in the Birmingham commuter belt.

By the time the last CPF employees were paid off, in April 1971, Merthyr was faced with a setback on a larger scale. Teddington Aircraft Controls was not only the second largest factory (at least, when at its peak) but the pride of the town and symbol of its footing in the new era of sophisticated technology. TAC made high-precision equipment for aircraft, including thermostats, hot-air valves, de-icers, and gauges delicate enough to check the temperature inside a turbine blade. TAC not only made them, indeed, but designed and developed them from general specifications.

Over a period of four or five years, it became evident that things were going badly for TAC. New projects were started, but the men responsible were advised not to take them seriously, and they didn't come to fruition. The payroll was cut by degrees to 700, less than half what it had once been. The reasons are complicated, and are linked ultimately to the troubles besetting the British aircraft industry. But heads of working departments, when I met them in the queue at the Employment Exchange, spoke angrily of bad management and asserted that TAC could be a bustling concern today had it been run properly. On one occasion, I was told, thirty draughtsmen were paid off on a Friday and one of them was requested on the following Monday to work on an urgent blueprint – as a freelance paid only for the time that it took.

Early in 1971, the AUEW branch in the factory gave notice of a strike for a wage increase. The management posted a notice to say that, if the strike took place, the factory would close. It was therefore postponed for a week, but no negotiations were opened and the engineers, so union leaders say, were virtually forced to go on strike. During these events, TAC was bought up by United Gas Industries, and it was announced that the Merthyr factory would be closed and the work transferred to UGI's plant at Streatham.

There was an outcry, and not merely because of what the closure would do to Merthyr's unemployment figures. The skilled men at TAC were much more than a labour force; they were a team with years of experience in working together and exchanging ideas. Such a team can be broken up at a stroke, but can be replaced only with difficulty. TAC might be a lame duck financially, it was argued, but the team was a national asset and the nation's responsibility was to keep it together, using the factory – which is an excellent building – for whatever development work the nation most needs. The workers elected deputations to put their case to Department of Industry officials in Cardiff and London, and lobbied the Prime Minister when he came to Cardiff. Then they paid £120 to place an advertisement in *The Times,* appealing to some company to seize the opportunity. It read: 'We can give you what we have given our present employers for twenty-five years or more – a high degree of workmanship and skill, conscientious effort and loyalty. All we ask is a company who can appreciate these virtues and promise a reasonably secure future.' The appeal went unheard, Whitehall declined to help, and men who must be among the most highly trained in British industry were left to draw the dole.

For some, there was the option of a move to Streatham – if they could cope with buying a new house at London prices. And a few drew on their savings and took out mortgages. Reconnaissance trips to the UGI works, however, left an impression that carrying on TAC work there was an impractical scheme; the specialized labour wasn't being, and apparently couldn't be, recruited and the buildings were unsuitable. This hunch was correct. Within three months, UGI had disposed of the outstanding contracts to Normalair Garrett Ltd, a subsidiary of Westland Helicopters, with a factory at Yeovil. It happened that Westland, at just this time, decided to close its works at Hayes, near London, and offer some of the workers jobs at Yeovil too. So competition at Yeovil was going to be stiff – both for jobs and for houses. Scenting the influx from Hayes, estate agents in the quiet Somersetshire town revised their prices so that moving there from Merthyr was even more costly than moving to Streatham.

Dismissals at TAC began in August 1971, and the factory

closed its doors in November. By then, there was more bad news for Merthyr. Triang, third in size among local industries, was in the hands of the liquidator.

This was an event to astonish every parent who had ever bought a Christmas present. Triang belongs to the Lines group of companies, and its products – Triang toy cars, Meccano, Dinky toys, Pedigree prams – are the outstanding names in their field. So was Rolls-Royce, however. With the national economy in the doldrums, profits had been declining for three years and the group found itself short of liquid assets. The lethal blow was struck by President Nixon, whose stringent measures to protect the dollar compelled a big American company to withdraw from an agreed investment in the Lines group. The banks refused further credit, and the group went into voluntary liquidation. Three factories and 2,000 workers were menaced, 700 of the workers being in Merthyr.

I was given this explanation at the head office in Merton, at a time when I tended to look at the world through Merthyr eyes. In ten minutes' stroll before my appointment, I must have passed enough factories to wipe out the Merthyr unemployment problem twice over. Outside the Triang factory, a notice declared:

We are Not Closing Down!
We are Continuing in Business as Normal.
We urgently require
Men and Women
to fill a wide Range of
VACANCIES

Even if there was no possibility of closing down, the management would never think of displaying such a notice outside the Merthyr factory, whose workers don't have the reckless London habit of changing their jobs, and where the occasional vacancies can always be filled by a phone call to the Employment Exchange. In the office, an executive assured me that the liquidator was keeping the factories going and no redundancies were being ordered; there was good reason to hope that the business would be saved, and the decision would be taken by the end of the year.

In January 1972, as I was preparing this book for the press, I learned that Triang had in fact been saved. The company has been taken over by a large consortium and is to stay in production. For Merthyr, it is indeed a mercy.

The TAC disaster and the Triang liquidation were the obvious talking-points while I was in Merthyr, and the remaining hopes of the citizens – indeed, the hopes of the redundant too – centred on the Hoover factory. Its contribution to the employment total, at 2,200, was much the biggest in the manufacturing field and exceeded only by that of the National Coal Board. The universal view was that, if Hoover's went, Merthyr would be in deep trouble and it would be no exaggeration to speak of mass unemployment. The recovery and the transformation – based on the arrival of Hoover, Triang and TAC in 1946-49 – would be a closed chapter. Merthyr as a centre of modern engineering would follow Merthyr as a steel town into the shadows.

The possibility was awful, but not out of the question. Hoover's had been rocky and had sharply pruned its payroll before, notably in 1965. On such occasions, it is the management's practice to invite each workshop to reduce its strength, say, by a quarter; it's left to personal discussion who is to 'volunteer' to walk out into the snow like Captain Oates, so that in the literal sense there are never any redundancies.

Fortunately, in 1971 it was demonstrable even to the casual eye that the Hoover factory was unlikely to close, for the builders were putting the finishing touches to a large extension, representing an investment of £3,000,000. Rather surprisingly, this meant only 200 new jobs; I heard it suggested that work in the old building would be thinned out. Visiting Merthyr, Hoover's chairman told the press that the extension 'will take some time to digest before the company can plan further expansion'. There might be opportunities in Europe, he said, but 'market conditions have never been fiercer than today . . . we must keep our costs to a minimum.' On the best prognosis, Hoover's are not going to make up for the TAC shut-down or solve the Merthyr unemployment problem.

In the economic climate of this year, with the condition of major firms varying between caution and collapse, it can well be imagined that smaller undertakings are struggling to survive. A complete survey in Merthyr would have shown some cutting the payroll by a quarter or a third, some putting their workers on short time, some frankly giving up. A fellow-guest at the New Inn revealed himself as a liquidator, taking charge of a factory (fifty workers) for its final month. I asked him if bankruptcies were on the increase, compared with a couple of years ago. He said that he didn't really know; he had been working in industry, had been made redundant, and had been lucky enough to land a job with the Official Receiver.

Meanwhile, white-collar employment – always scanty for a town of Merthyr's size – is equally on the wane. Girls were vainly seeking work months after getting good marks in the shorthand and typing course at the College of Further Education, whereas in any previous year they had been placed by September. In recent years the Gas Board, the Electricity Board, and the Water Board have all moved their offices from Merthyr to other towns, such as Pontypridd. It's a wounding denigration of Merthyr as a regional centre.

And emigration continues. Out of 106 people who had secured jobs in the last month analysed at the Employment Exchange, 52 had found them outside Merthyr. The great majority, naturally, were within daily travelling distance. But ten were in Cardiff (where the persons concerned may or may not go to live), three in London, two in High Wycombe, two in the Midlands. Other people leave Merthyr without telling the Employment Exchange, if they get jobs fixed up by relatives who had departed earlier.

The Manager of the Employment Exchange remarked to me that there are not so many young unemployed men in Merthyr as one might expect, given the undeniably diminishing opportunities. Some, he said, took unskilled work even if they had good educational qualifications, hoping that it would be only a stop-gap. This was confirmed to me by older men to whom I chatted as they waited to sign on. As they explained, a skilled man – especially if he was on earnings-related benefit – wouldn't find it worth while to take a job at £15 a week, but a youngster would.

But, the Manager admitted sadly, another factor is that young men are leaving the town. It is confidence that is lacking: confidence, or simply hope. Being an honest man, the Manager agreed that confidence isn't to be created by pep-talks or promises; maybe in some places, but not in Merthyr. When there are opportunities there will be confidence, and not before.

What is surprising to the visitor – surprising and moving – is that so many people remain loyal to Merthyr. They recall the revival of 1946, and explain how easily it could be made to happen again, given a Government that cares enough and finds the will to act. Or, quite simply, they assert that Merthyr will survive because it must.

Now and then, all the same, the bitterness breaks through. 'I worked for Vickers-Armstrong in Dartford from 1935 to 1938,' an unemployed man told me. 'I came back to Merthyr. I must have been bloody daft.'

In January 1972 – the month that saw the national unemployment total rise to over a million for the first time since the war – Merthyr Tydfil had 1,817 on the dole, including 124 women, 85 youths under the age of 21, and 57 girls. The percentage of all insured workers was 7.7, compared with a national average of 4.3. For a number of reasons – principally the reprieve of Triang – it wasn't as bad as had been feared. Figures of over 10% were recorded elsewhere in Wales, as well as in Scotland and Northern Ireland. But there was no sign of an upturn, no prospect of new opportunities. Unemployment of this order, so far as anyone could see, was something that Merthyr would have to go on enduring.

10

Mr D. W. Howells, headmaster of Afon Taf comprehensive school at Troedirhiw, has good reason to be a proud man. After teaching for thirty years in more or less antiquated buildings, he was appointed to the new headship when Merthyr Tydfil went over to the comprehensive system, and urged to help in the design of the new school to be built on the bank of the Taf. Seldom, in fact, has there been such close co-operation between headmaster and architect. Mr Howells can point to various features on which he insisted, such as small laboratories for sixth-formers so that they don't have to dismantle an experiment when a junior class uses the lab. He also ensured that anyone can get everywhere in the school without going out into the rain. Making a whirlwind tour of Afon Taf with the enthusiastic headmaster, I saw that it has everything that money can buy or ingenuity suggest: language labs, closed-circuit television, and even a stationary car for driving lessons. So Mr Howells is proud of his school, proud of his boys and girls, and even – this is much rarer – proud of his local education authority.

For Merthyr, ever since it became a borough, had adhered passionately, and stubbornly when necessary, to the creed that education is a vital investment in a community's future. Councillors – often men who themselves went down the pit in boyhood, and who know all about rickets and nutritional deficiencies – speak with fervour when they declare that nothing is too good for the children. While I was writing this book, Merthyr was in the news mainly because it was the only education authority in England and Wales to defy Mrs Thatcher's ban on free milk in primary schools. Having met some of the Councillors, I haven't the slightest doubt that they meant it when they said they were ready to go to prison on the issue.

Mrs Thatcher, however, was far from being the first Minister to learn the meaning of Merthyr determination. Back in 1921, the borough asked for a secondary school and was told by the Board of Education (as it then was) that the request could not be met. Merthyr's reply was to discover a collection of wooden buildings standing empty on Salisbury Plain, buy them from the Army which had used them during the 1914-18 war, cart them off to Quaker's Yard, recruit teachers, and get the school in business before Whitehall knew what was happening. In the depression years, as I've recorded, economy in education was a saving that the bankrupt borough refused to make. Elementary education to the age of fourteen, with only a handful of working-class children getting scholarships, was then the rule. But in Merthyr during the 1930s, almost one child in four reached a secondary school at public expense. There were many far richer towns and counties that could not say as much.

When relative prosperity returned, education was the first priority and Merthyr had the extraordinary figure of 45% of its pupils going to grammar schools. (To be accurate, this would have been amazing anywhere in England but was only a bit better than normal in Wales.) A further 20% of the age-group took vocational courses at the College of Further Education, for which the town built a fine modern building beside the Taf. Only about one pupil in three, therefore, was going into the labour market at the minimum legal age. Broadening its scope and raising its standards, the College will rank as a Technical College from 1972.

When the comprehensive idea took hold, Merthyr made the change with a speed that, once again, put many wealthier authorities to shame. Nor was it done by putting new names on old buildings. In the coming school year there will be four comprehensives, three of them purpose-built: Afon Taf was completed in 1967, a Catholic comprehensive is also in use, and another state comprehensive on the commanding hillside of Gurnos is almost ready. Only one comprehensive will continue to be housed in former grammar-school and secondary-modern buildings – but it would be a pity to give up teaching in Cyfarthfa Castle, whose occupation for that purpose was in the nature of a conquest.

All this goes to explain why Mr Howells is a proud man. To describe him as a happy man, however, would be far from the truth. Glaring across his desk, he declared: 'It's tragic to be headmaster of a school like this.' The tragedy is this: the better an education that a boy gets, the surer it is that he will either be unemployed or leave Merthyr. (For girls, this is even truer.) Future scientists, future technologists, future arts graduates, future teachers – they all go sooner or later, and very few come back.

It's a long tradition to ask the stranger what is the principal export of Wales and, after rejecting answers like 'coal' and 'steel', to announce emphatically: 'Brains!' Long before it became a catch-phrase for the drift across the Atlantic, the 'brain drain' was a reality as the Great Western's expresses rattled through the Severn Tunnel. Generation after generation, the boys who emerged at Paddington went on to become inventors, surgeons, professors, architects, civil service knights. It was a cause of pride, but of bitterness too; for the boys were lost to Wales, making no contribution to the life of their own country, finding no outlet in it for their talents. The world was enriched by what they did, but Wales was not. And still it goes on. No other region of the United Kingdom, in proportion to its population, produces so much professional and educationally qualified manpower as Wales. No other region, except the Northeast, is so poor in opportunities for that class of manpower. Moreover, if the way is difficult for young people with A-levels or degrees, it is almost equally difficult –

considering the numbers – for young people who aim at apprenticeships and entry into skilled trades.

Opportunities of this kind were a welcome aspect of the full-employment policy pursued by the Labour Government of 1945-51, which did so much to give Merthyr a new chance. Consider, for instance, the biography of Councillor John Reddy, now chairman of Merthyr's Housing Committee. He left school during that period at the age of fifteen and had a couple of blind-alley jobs, one in a butcher's shop and one labelling bottles in a soda-pop factory. Then he heard of a Government-subsidized scheme for training boys in the building trade, and became a plasterer's apprentice. It changed his life; he now has his own small business, mostly adding bathrooms and doing similar conversion work on old houses, and incidentally has built a very attractive house for himself. In any case, he can always earn a living at his trade. But the scheme was wound up in the 1950s. Now, Mr Reddy wants it started up again as a weapon against unemployment. The trainees could work on building Council houses, a continuing programme in Merthyr. A house would cost £5,000 instead of £4,000 to build, he admits – 'but never mind that, you'd be taking a hundred lads off the dole.' He has pressed his case at the Welsh Office and in Whitehall, so far without any success. As things are, all that the Council can manage on its own resources is a training scheme for maintenance work. Recently, an advertisement for five apprentices brought in 92 applications.

Unemployment among young people is, in many ways, the most disturbing element in Merthyr's present situation. When I inquired for what in most towns is called the Youth Employment Office, I found that in Merthyr it is hopefully entitled the Careers Office and housed in the College of Further Education. The Careers Officer turned out to be a very worried man. He explained that his records always show a peak figure of about 200 job-seekers in August, after the year has ended in the schools and the College. Normally he reduces it pretty quickly; for instance, it was down to 46 in October 1970. But in October 1971 it was an obstinate 139 – actually a shade higher than in September, which showed that some youths who'd found work had already been made redundant. Firms that take apprentices every autumn, including Hoover's, were cutting the numbers; the Gas Board, for the first time in the Careers Officer's memory, was taking none at all. And he named a firm—as a matter of fact, not in Merthyr but in the Rhymney Valley – which had just dismissed all its apprentices regardless of the stage they had reached in their training, and regardless of having to pay the Government levy which penalises firms without apprentices.

A sardonic sidelight on the outlook for the younger generation of South Wales appeared at the end of 1971 when, on the initiative of the Cardiff YMCA, a working party on 'the problems of the young unemployed' brought together representatives of youth and community organizations.

The agreed report stated: 'It should be an accepted responsibility of all secondary schools to prepare pupils for the reality of life (including possible unemployment) which they will have to face on their leaving school, and it should be recognized that all pupils, those academically gifted as well as those less well endowed, have a need for such guidance.' Later, the report suggested 'recreational and creative activities' and 'non-vocational courses' for unemployed young people. The purpose, it was explained, would be 'to help them to make the most of their personal resources, so that they might maintain a more dignified attitude to life in spite of their unemployment'.

True, the report concluded by declaring: 'The only long-term answer is a return to full employment', and the working party added its voice to all those in Wales putting the responsibility primarily on the Government. There's a depressing ring, all the same, to the word 'long-term' and to the whole idea that the role of the school is to prepare boys

and girls for adjustment to unemployment. It isn't, I feel
certain, how Mr Howells sees his job. A week on the dole is
a long time for those who are starting out in life.

11

Since I came back from Merthyr, several friends have asked me. 'What's it really like there?' I have been careful not to reply with adjectives like 'horrifying' or 'heart-breaking'. Unemployment in itself – the rejection of a man's energies and skills, the growing sense of disappointment as one unsuccessful application follows another, the sheer stupid waste – is bad enough without any need for me to paint a picture of despair or hunger. 1971 is not 1931, neither for the town nor indeed for the unemployed themselves. A television team might find nothing to film: certainly no gaunt faces, no patched clothes or leaking shoes, no under-nourished children. While it was a shock merely to drive through Merthyr in the depression years, it would be quite easy now to spend a day there and have no idea that anything was wrong. If the sun is shining, the men in good suits and light raincoats on the benches outside the Employment Exchange might well be waiting for the pubs to open. If the stranger notices anything unusual, it's probably that men wear white shirts and ties and women wear hats rather more in Merthyr than in most places.

When all this is said, however, anyone who makes more than a short stay will get an impression of a community without much money to spare. There are, as I've said, few small factories or workshops owned by local people; the big factories go outside Merthyr for their sub-contracting, whereas a big factory in the Midlands normally gets its bits and pieces a mile away, and this local supply network is an important prop to prosperity and full employment. There are not many laundrettes and dry-cleaners in Merthyr, not many small builders and decorators, not many garages, not many cafés and snack-bars. The Hing Hong in the High Street serves an excellent three-course lunch for 31p, but it's often impossible to get a seat – both at midday and in the evening – because it is the only real restaurant in the town.

Even in the depression, so a man who'd managed to hold on to his job told me, Merthyr had five cinemas, five dance-halls, a theatre, variety at the Temperance Hall, and a roller-skating rink. If you could afford to take a girl out at all, you could go to a dance-hall for one and sixpence including refreshments. Not much of this remains. Of course, changing tastes and television have cut swathes in away-from-home entertainment everywhere; yet the choice of where to spend an evening out in Merthyr is unusually limited. The Theatre Royal has resigned itself to bingo; the rink has been demolished. A dance-hall in the High Street, the only one I could find, has a notice saying 'Closed until further notice' – possibly the consequence of an earlier notice which reads: 'The wearing of casual jeans is not permitted. Collars and ties must be worn at all times.' Two cinemas survive, both ageing buildings in need of a coat of paint. The ABC (or Castle) is one of those old-style picture palaces that evoke memories of James Cagney, creaking seats, and subdued cries of 'Stop it, now!' from the back row. There must be about a thousand seats in the stalls, at 30p. When I went on a Wednesday night to see '2001 Space Odyssey', twenty-six of them were occupied. And if that's an evening out in Merthyr, how about Troedirhiw?

The High Street is as narrow as ever – the trams that once ran through it must have been a menace to pedestrians – but it causes no traffic problems. Even when a delivery van stops and takes up half the width of the roadway, there's only a brief hold-up. In the side-streets, people often walk or stand chatting in the middle; you can find a parking-place almost anywhere and stay all day for nothing. In this respect, a week in Merthyr is a delight for a Londoner – but it must be true, though I've no figures, that car ownership is below average. Mostly, the people who do have cars take them to work. With most of the railway lines closed and the bus services inadequate, a car is almost a necessity for a man with a job in another valley. Yet I've never seen anything in Merthyr that could be called a rush-hour.

The old houses are, in general, owner-occupied; they sell for about £2,000 if modernized, for as little as £500 if not. How many are modernized, I'm not sure. The Chairman of the Housing Committee told me that they 'tend to lack amenities'; so, he added, do the houses built by the Council under what's called in Merthyr 'the 1890 Act'—the first legislation to authorize local-authority housing. The 1961 census showed that 51% of houses in Merthyr had no bath and 42% had no hot water. A great deal of use has been made of improvement grants since then, but it's safe to say that the 1971 figures (not yet available) will show Merthyr as still trailing behind national standards. By comparison with most parts of Britain, and indeed with the Vale of Glamorgan, very few new houses for owner-occupation are being built in Merthyr – scarcely any, in fact, except a rather nasty 'estate' at Heolgerrig. For this there are some good reasons, such as the effective programme of Council housing, and a natural attachment to the solid and attractive old houses. But another reason is the falling population, and yet another must surely be lack of cash.

One sometimes hears the question: 'What is Merthyr (or Wales, or Scotland) doing to help itself?' To accept this as the question that really matters is to concede just what shouldn't be conceded; the real solutions must be in national planning and a general quickening of the economy. If baiting Merthyr's hook sufficed, one would need only to recall those token rents on the industrial estate and those fifty thousand pounds spent on adapting buildings for a firm that went away after five years. If words could work the charm, the prose style of the Merthyr Development Committee's glossy brochure – 'proud and vigorous County Borough . . . loyal, adaptable workers . . . ample opportunities for the far-sighted and enterprising . . . the pulse of new life and energy beats out the potential of the future' – ought to soften the stoniest heart.

Still, the answer to the question is that Merthyr has made a strenuous effort to turn itself into a spick-and-span modern town. In addition to those 5,000 post-war Council houses, there's a transformation down where the old ironworks once poisoned the Taf: a new fire station, new bus depot, new office building for the Department of Health and Social Security, new shopping precinct on the Coventry model complete with gently inclined walkways and abstract sculpture. If anything, there has been an excess of enthusiasm. The spacious new 'neighbourhoods' have jettisoned what was really neighbourly about the old close-packed streets, and could be in Slough or Eltham as well as in Wales. The shopping-power of Merthyr families evidently can't sustain the High Street as well as the precinct, and in five minutes' walk along the former you can count sixteen empty premises. But even the miscalculations have a moving quality, when one senses the determination to refute that damning phrase, 'a dying town'.

Ultimately, a town is only as big as the opportunities that it offers, and the basic opportunities are those which provide a wide variety of work. I referred in the last chapter to the 'brain drain' which has taken so many trained and talented young people from Wales to England. But there is also a local brain drain, a movement from the rural areas and the mining valleys to Cardiff or Swansea. For Cardiff and Swansea are cities. They have universities, research centres, big hospitals with specialist departments, daily newspapers, television studios, assize courts, large office blocks. They have less of everything than London has, but a good deal more than a town like Merthyr. By comparison with the Welsh past, they are flourishing places.

This contrast between opportunity in one place and stagnation or actual decline in another is the most heated issue in Wales today. It is not a simple issue. No one wants residence permits or internal passports on the model of Czarist Russia; a certain number of ambitious young people, individually, will always be on the move from towns of 50,000 population to towns of 500,000, and from anywhere and everywhere to the great cities. But the argument as it's put by people like Mr Howells is that there should be a genuine choice, that the man who wants to stay in his home town and work to the full stretch of his ability and training should be able to do so. This choice, at present, scarcely exists. Before it can exist, national policy must stimulate the development of what, for a generation, have been Development Areas on paper.

Why, exactly, is Aldermaston – not just a bomb factory nowadays, but Britain's principal centre of advanced scientific work – in the London exurbanite belt? Why, when inner London gets too crowded, does the Admiralty settle in Bath and the Royal Mint move to Llantrisant in the Vale of Glamorgan? Why is the Road Research Laboratory at Slough and the Royal Aircraft Establishment at Farnborough? Why are there new universities on the fringes of Brighton, Canterbury, Colchester, Guildford and Uxbridge? Why would it sound funny to the decision-makers to suggest that something of the kind should be at Merthyr?

In a Council house on the Gurnos estate, a girl with a certificate from the College of Further Education and no job flared up and said to me: 'People think we live in caves down here.' Through the neglect, Merthyr senses not only indifference but contempt. It is an unhealthy state of mind; but what is healthy about the situation?

12

On the page of the Automobile Association's handbook which lists Melton Mowbray, Mere and Mevagissey, there is no entry for Merthyr Tydfil. (Why it should be a joke for a tourist to make his way to Merthyr, when it's on the edge of a National Park, is another good question.) Working with a map, however, one discovers that Merthyr is 178 miles from London, 105 from Birmingham, and 59 from Bristol. Words like 'remote' scarcely seem justified. But ever since Merthyr became a problem town, industrialists have cited 'transport difficulties' as a reason for refusing to settle there.

For old railwaymen, the quiet that surrounds Merthyr station is melancholy. Decades of decline from the heyday of the railway age culminated in the Beeching Plan, particularly ruthless in South Wales. The line to Cardiff – the only one that survives – has been reduced from double to single track; the sheds, where about thirty engines used to be kept and serviced, no longer exist; freight traffic is virtually zero; the station itself, shown in old prints as a noble structure with an arching glass roof, is now a cube of red brick that could be mistaken for a public lavatory, from which a handful of passengers emerge once an hour. The dwindling of the railway, in fact, has made its contribution to unemployment. However, the railway age is over for good, and the new industries like Hoover's moved their output in lorries from the start. If it's a question of transport difficulties, roads are what matter.

The road from Merthyr to Cardiff, which has street-lights all the way, is simply the main street of one village after another. The road itself is narrow and the pavements are like those of a picturesque old quarter such as the sixth *arrondissement* of Paris; the noise that shakes the houses when heavy lorries grind past makes the vicinity of London Airport seem like a country churchyard. In my experience, it's quite an achievement to drive the twenty-five miles in under an hour. Plans for a new road have been 'under active consideration' for over twenty years. Now the first section of the road is being built – starting from the Cardiff end, naturally, not the Merthyr end – and it is due for completion in 1973.

The route through Abergavenny, taking Merthyr goods to the Midlands or London, is more important. Here too, construction began at the far end from Merthyr's point of view, with the M5 going southward out of Birmingham and the M50 branch motorway going westward as far as Ross. How to get from London to Ross still provides one of those arguments so dear to the British heart, with bad stretches whichever choice you make. After Ross, dual carriageway has now reached as far as Raglan, with a remaining stretch of eight miles of country lane from there to Abergavenny.

Once on the Welsh plateau, you strike the Heads of the Valleys Road whose importance to Merthyr has caused me to mention it several times. This road too is the outcome of years of 'study' and 'consideration', along with table-thumping and Welsh eloquence from Merthyr deputations. It seems symbolic that it was eventually completed not as a dual carriageway but as a three-lane road – the only one to be built in Britain in recent times, after coroners up and down the land had deplored them as unsuited to modern traffic densities and speeds.

There is, however, a motorway from London to Wales. Although the M4 was delayed for years by the ingenious resistance of racehorse trainers in Berkshire, and opened at last only at the end of 1971, it was always on the planners' maps as a major section of the British motorway network. It goes to Newport, Cardiff, and the Vale of Glamorgan, and will be a great help to the development of those places.

The planners have two ideas for development in Wales. Both are viewed in Merthyr and the valleys with as much enthusiasm as a scheme for plastic plates might arouse in the Potteries or a lemonade campaign in Beaujolais. One is called Severnside and would involve creating an industrial belt somewhere along the coast. Although a study is being made at considerable expense, no early decisions are likely and it's even doubtful whether 'Severnside' means the Welsh side of the Severn estuary or both sides. (Or just the English side, some Welshmen predict acidly.) The other idea, for a New Town at Llantrisant, is at a much more advanced stage. The area has been defined, the Designation Order – which is the crucial step – will probably be made in 1972, and some industrialists are showing keen interest. The Royal Mint is already there; this, taken together with some early grubbing by bulldozers, has inspired Merthyr wits to describe Llantrisant as the Hole with the Mint.

In terms of town and country planning, there are several weighty objections to Severnside. Industry is present in some strength along the estuary already, notably in the shape of the big steelworks at Llanwern. The belt of lowland countryside isn't very large, and some of it is taken up by holiday resorts and caravan sites; some, also, by good farming land of which Wales has little to spare. 'God made the valleys for industry and the coast for enjoyment,' Mr Howells informed me, and this seems as good an interpretation of His intentions as any. Given the restricted space, development could scarcely fail to turn Cardiff and Newport, hitherto fairly compact towns, into sprawling conurbations with intricate traffic problems. Wales, in fact, would be imitating on its own scale the drift to the south-east that, in the context of Britain as a whole, everyone deplores.

Llantrisant, more particularly, is as choice a piece of anti-planning as one could well find. It is only ten miles from Cardiff, whereas the other New Towns are at least twenty miles from London, Liverpool or Birmingham. These towns were designed to take industry out of the cities, a function which has no relevance in the case of Cardiff. It was central to the whole conception that a man who lived in, say, Crawley should also work in Crawley. He wasn't supposed to commute to London; to the extent that New Town residents do so, a partial failure of the plan has to be recognized. At a range of ten miles, Llantrisant is bound to be filled with Cardiff commuters. Houses can be built quicker than factories, and Llantrisant could soon – and irremediably – deserve the name that has been anathema to planners in modern times: a dormitory town. Actually, it is being envisaged from the outset – in flat contradiction of the original New Town theory – that Llantrisant will provide housing for people with jobs in Cardiff. The New Town is being created at least as much for housing reasons as for industrial reasons: so I was told in Cardiff by officials of the Department of Trade and Industry – not by officials of the Department of the Enrivonment's housing division, who might be expected to urge such considerations. Clearly, it wouldn't take long to fill up the open country between Cardiff and Llantrisant, and another dirty word of the bad old days before planning may soon make its reappearance: ribbon development. Nowadays, I think, it's called linear planning.

In Merthyr eyes, the case against Severnside and Llantrisant is much simpler. Development in the Vale or on the coast will be at the expense of development in the valleys. Nobody would object to the attraction of new industry to both regions (Cardiff has unemployment too) but nobody believes that it is contemplated. At least, there is no sign of a study for the valleys. A choice is being made, and once again Merthyr is not among the chosen.

The officials I've mentioned, in giving me an outline of the Department of Trade and Industry's attitudes, wasted no time on bromides. Investment grants for development Areas have been abolished by the present Government, and the first point made by these officials was that these grants had never solved the problem anyway. To my mind this was like saying that, since insulin doesn't cure diabetes but merely keeps the diabetic alive, one might as well stop prescribing it; but I wasn't there to argue. Their next point, however, was indisputable: that the hope of better times for any part of Britain depends on the national and international economic climate. About the said climate, being civil servants and not politicians, they made no breezy forecasts. I then remarked that Merthyr always has unemployment above the national average, even in good times, and asked what, in their view, could be done to put this right. They replied that it was awfully hard to think of anything.

They went on to explain that the M4 route is bound to be the number one preference for industrialists considering a location in Wales. Their plans were based on the assumption that expansion would take place in a belt eight miles wide in the Vale of Glamorgan. When jobs were available in this belt, workers would come from Merthyr and the valleys, and in the course of time would move to homes in the Vale. As they put it, there was a natural drift of population away from the valleys – or if it wasn't natural (we had a few minutes of semantics about this word) at any rate it was irreversible. And I was assured that concern over the falling population of a town like Merthyr was confined to the older generation, and in particular to councillors worrying about the yield of the rates.

All of this takes us back to the two schools of thought which emerged in depression days, one maintaining that Merthyr could be revived by new industry and the other that it was a hopeless case. It wasn't difficult, as I drove back along the wretched road up the valley, to grasp that the second school of thought predominates in the Department of Trade and Industry.

But if I had been there to argue, what reply could I have made? If one rejects the verdict of inevitable decline for Merthyr one must have an alternative in clear terms of policies and methods.

In the first place, when the economic recovery of Britain

does happen – and it would be outside my scope to say how it can be achieved – it must be something different from the boom of the Macmillan era, when the search for quick profits decided which industries and which regions were to flourish. As in the immediate post-war years, the Government must use conscious policy, control and discrimination to make development move in certain directions and not in others.

Secondly, the industries developed in Merthyr must include industries centred in Merthyr and representing a large investment in plant: industries that would not be moved away, and that would never be shut down unless we get another depression like that of the 'thirties. An example would be the manufacture of heavy machinery.

Thirdly, the employment in Merthyr of skilled and professional manpower is an essential. It would end the injustice of the 'brain drain', it would do more than anything else to create an atmosphere of confidence, and it would introduce purchasing power based on high earnings. This must be done by deliberate policy too; one can't rely again on the lucky chance that one of the factories which went to Merthyr was TAC with its opportunities for skill. It can be done through the choice of industry, and it can be done too through the siting of research institutes and laboratories. In this sphere – at least, in enough of this sphere to help Merthyr – the controlling authority is the Department of Education and Science and there are no private interests to be persuaded.

Fourthly, although investment grants ought to be restored, it is honest to recognize that they never wholly solved the problems of the Development Areas and that they are unlikely to be so useful again as they were in the exceptional conditions of the aftermath of war. Governments, Labour as well as Tory, have always balked at direction of industry, accepting the argument that it would entail direction of labour. Perhaps it would, if industry were directed to an area of labour shortage or full employment; but nobody is suggesting that. An industry directed to Merthyr would find labour ready and waiting. And once the industry is established, labour moves of its own accord; nobody orders immigrants to go to Bradford. To get the new factories to Merthyr, a tough use of the IDC system (without loopholes) might prove sufficient. But direction of industry is a measure of which a determined Government should be ready to avail itself.

But fifthly, the question of direction does not arise when Industry is publicly owned. When the nationalized boards set up new power stations or steel plants or railway workshops, they are deciding on a location in the same way as a private company. The trouble has been twofold: that they have acted only from commercial considerations, and no Government has obliged them to take account of social needs such as unemployment; and that public ownership has been confined to utilities, communications, and a couple of basic industries. There are many arguments for public ownership, in terms of Socialist doctrine, but one of them is certainly that it would be a major weapon to end the over-development of some regions and the under-development of others. It is hard to imagine a durable new future for a town like Merthyr without an extension of public ownership into a wide range of productive industry.

One may accept this kind of programme, or not. But my conviction is that those who do not accept it are accepting unemployment.

Part Two | The People

1

In the rest of this book, I shall introduce the reader individually to some of the unemployed of Merthyr Tydfil. I ought to say, to begin with, that these people were unemployed when I was staying in the town in November 1971. It is almost certain that some of them will have found jobs by the time that my book is published. If this made the book out of date, nobody would be better pleased than me. Unfortunately, other people in Merthyr who had jobs in November – people with different names, but in many ways similar to those whom I describe – will have become unemployed. The personal details vary; the predicament is the same.

This book, as most readers will have recognized by now, is a work of propaganda. (Goebbels accustomed the world to thinking that 'propaganda' means 'lies', but this was never so; the best propaganda is the truth.) I am not impartial about unemployment. I think it is an evil – a social evil, an economic evil, but above all a human evil. My aim is to awaken those who read the book to the reality of unemployment to such a degree that they feel it to be intolerable and resolve that it must be ended. This, I well know, is not easy.

In a superficial sense, the task may appear unnecessary. Practically everybody now knows that Britain has a million unemployed. Practically everybody agrees that this is a bad thing. There are people who think that the unemployed (or some of the unemployed) prefer to live idly on welfare benefits rather than work; or that 'ten men looking for nine jobs' makes for efficiency; or that complete security of employment leads to slackness. But even these people, in my experience, admit that a million out of work is too many. For one thing, there is not much sign of the efficiency. Britain remains – to recall the title of a topical paperback published almost ten years ago – a Stagnant Society. Five years have now passed since the so-called shake-out, caused by the economic squeeze of the autumn of 1966, ended the era of full employment. During those five years, our society has been more stagnant than ever. Britain's growth rate is the lowest of any industrialized nation; productivity, investment, re-equipment, inventiveness – all are at an unsatisfactory level. We don't even have lower prices, the one consolation of the depression of the 1930s. If anything, people work more slowly and cautiously and keep quiet if they have labour-saving ideas. Nobody wants to work himself out of a job.

About the 'efficiency' of unemployment, another point is worth making. Economists, not to mention politicians of both parties, have been telling us for years that we are 'paying ourselves more than we earn' – that individual incomes, and consequently purchasing power, are in excess of production. This, according to the conventional wisdom, is the cause of our recurrent problems and of inflation in particular. But if that is true, what could be worse than to pay people for doing nothing – to provide incomes that are balanced by no production whatever? The Redundancy Payments Act of 1965 (cynics may note that it was a prelude to the ending of full employment) compels the employer to pay out a lump sum, in general a week's wages for every year of work in the firm concerned, to each employee who is dismissed. Older workers who haven't changed their jobs have sometimes collected £1,000 or more. In humanitarian terms, and as a measure of social justice, this was an admirable innovation; to my mind, the solitary achievement of the Wilson Government. Social security benefits, too – although in many respects they leave much to be desired – are above the miserly levels of the 1930s. I am glad of all this, but I am also aware that it is an economic nonsense.

High unemployment, and the steady flow of redundancies, are in modern conditions a counterweight to everything that is meant by 'paying our way'.

Very well, then: it is a bad thing to have a million on the dole. It is a problem; more and more people are coming to consider it as Britain's most serious problem. Regrettably, that is part of the trouble. Poverty and refugees and war are problems too. Very easily, for those who are not personally involved, a problem can become an abstraction. What we are aware of, chiefly, is the size of the problem, and that is not the same thing as its urgency. We are aware of the unemployment total which appears once a month in the headlines and on the television screen. As we drew closer to it, the phrase 'a million unemployed' acquired a kind of hypnotic power. There were even sick jokes about the millionth unemployed man being invited to lunch at 10 Downing Street.

Certainly, the size of the problem is important. The nation is poorer in every sense, and its ailments are graver, with a million unemployed than with 500,000. But being unemployed, like being poor and being a refugee and being hit by a bullet, is something that happens to a human being. It is as bad for him whether he is one of 500,000 or one of a million.

As a propagandist, I am sharply aware of this aspect of the matter. It used to be the practice to publish daily figures of deaths on the road during Christmas and other Bank Holiday periods. Everyone agreed that the figures were too high – there was a problem. Then, one December, the *Daily Mirror* printed a double page of photographs; these were the actual men, women and children who had been killed during Christmas, who had been alive and smiling when they faced the camera and were now dead. The result was a shock of horror. That is the reason for Part Two of this book.

But I feel the intimate reality of unemployment, I hope, in other ways than as a propagandist. The unemployed –

the people of whom I shall be writing – are not an abstraction to me; they are not photographs; they are remembered faces and voices. If I hear that one of them has found work, I shall be personally relieved. Of course, I claim no particular virtue in this; it would be the same for anyone who had the same experience as me.

In other words, I care about the unemployed – about the unemployed of Merthyr in particular, because I can give names and faces to them, and therefore also about the unemployed of Liverpool and Clydeside and Belfast, whose lives and feelings are much the same. But does Mr Heath care? Or Mr Barber, or Sir John Eden? Or the MP for an affluent Home Counties constituency, or the editor of a quality newspaper? Or the average middle-class Londoner who is securely employed as doctor or lawyer, university lecturer or civil servant, restaurant manager or stockbroker? Or you, dear reader, if you know no one personally who is on the dole?

These questions may seem harsh, or in bad taste. I can only speak for myself. I know that I care more about hunger in India than about hunger in Peru, because I have been in India – the faces and the voices live with me – and I haven't been to Peru. It ought not to be so, as a matter of principle, but it is so. Personal involvement – if only that of the visitor, the inquirer – is the catalyst of sympathy.

In my first chapter, I used the word *they* as it is used in Merthyr: *they*, the ruling class, the authorities, the Tories. Deep in the mind of Merthyr is the belief that *they* do not care about unemployment – do not care enough to be angry, or ashamed, or grieved, as people are who come close to it. This is not because of any illusion that *they* are monsters, incapable of ordinary human feeling; Merthyr people have more sense than to imagine that. It is simply because *they* are far away, living an utterly different kind of life.

One becomes aware of this difference most keenly when one discusses the duration of unemployment. In middle-class London it is one kind of discussion, and in Merthyr it is quite another. We know – at least, all the experts say – that there will be no upturn in the economy, and consequently no remedy for unemployment, until the autumn of 1972 at the earliest. It is possible to state this as an objective fact, regrettable no doubt, but without emotional force. But in Merthyr 'no upturn in the economy' is not an abstraction. It means 'no job for Harry at number five'. Harry will become poorer, because his earnings-related benefit will run out. Harry's wife will not buy a new coat. Harry's children will not go to the seaside.

With every month of unemployment, there is an increase in the size of what commentators call the 'hard core' – people who have been out of work for more than eight weeks, and are therefore assumed to have a real problem. This is a vital difference between Britain's present situation and the position when we have 'full employment', by which we mean fewer than 250,000 out of work. In those conditions, most of the unemployed belong to the soft flesh, or whatever the opposite to hard core may be in this fruity metaphor. A man loses his job, perhaps because a firm has been badly managed and has failed, perhaps because it is going to move and he doesn't want to move with it. He knows that he can get a similar job, and he has no intention of filling a vacancy in a different or worse-paid kind of work. He is in no hurry; he looks round and picks up rumours, he enjoys an unexpected break, he gets pleasure out of catching up on the gardening and being with the children for a couple of weeks. If he meets his friends, he says that he's changing his job, and this is in effect the truth. He feels no sense of failure, certainly no shame. It would be going too far in the direction of complacency to say that, in a boom year like 1964, all the 250,000 unemployed were in this happy position – not in Merthyr, anyway – but a good many of them were.

When a man has been out of work for a considerable period, and when the level of unemployment is high, everything is different. The feeling of freedom or of relaxation, as he walks down the street in working hours, vanishes. Instead, he has a feeling of being lost. He has been deprived of his place in the world, and doesn't know how to regain it. If he is a skilled worker, there comes a difficult moment when he decides to take whatever work is going, be it delivering milk or sweeping up leaves in the park. It is difficult because he may well be abandoning for ever his status as lathe-operator or draughtsman, with all the interest and sense of achievement that the work provides. The doctor or lawyer, who knows that he will always be a doctor or a lawyer, needs to make a vast effort of imagination to put himself in this situation. But later, perhaps, a worse moment comes: the unskilled work isn't available either; the man who has reconciled himself to take whatever is going finds that nothing is going.

Suppose, however, that our unemployed man was an unskilled worker in the first place. He has no claim on any kind of job, no priority, no particular place in the world. From the start, from the day he registered at the Employment Exchange, he has declared himself ready to do anything; so, if he has found nothing after eight weeks, it means that there is nothing to be found. There is no reason to expect that the right vacancy will occur in time, for there is no right vacancy. There are no grounds for hope; there is nothing to rely on, except luck. And luck, as time goes by, seems as evasive as the treble-chance.

If eight weeks of unemployment makes you part of the hard core, what does six months make you? Or a year? Or two years? It can't be long now before some sociologist comes up with an analysis in depth of the long-term unemployed; but managers of Employment Exchanges know the answers already. They know that, the longer a man has been unemployed (and, of course, the older he is) the harder he is to place. They know that a change sets in, a true change in the personality. A man becomes 'institutionalized' in unemployment, as do other men in hospitals or prisons. Consciously, he wants to get out; at a deeper level, he doesn't. He has received too many rejections. He has come to accept that he is a failure and (at this deeper level) prefers not to be disturbed in that role. It is common, managers say, for such a man to be informed of a possible job and told to present himself for an interview, and to miss the appointment. This is the stage of final defeat. It is the ruin of a man.

In this deterioration, a large factor is sheer idleness. Few people have the inner resources to keep their minds active over long periods while no demands are made on them. The structure of an industrial society, in which a man cannot work unless he is given tools and machines to work with, has shaped us in a certain way, has made us different from the artisans and peasants who were our ancestors. What begins as leisure soon becomes sheer boredom. It is observable that, as time goes by, the unemployed make less and less use of it. The man who has been out of work for two months may perhaps be reading the books that he'd always meant to; the man who has been out of work for two years probably doesn't even read the newspaper.

When the organizers of the demonstration in Merthyr announced as their theme 'The Right to Work', they were striking a note of deep significance, especially in that kind of community. The right to work is more than the right to be occupied for eight hours a day. It is more than the right to earn, important though that obviously is. It is the right to *be* something – to be a miner, an engineer, a driver, a bricklayer. When you deprive a man of this, you deprive him of an essential in his life.

There is a scar across the mind of every man who went through long-term unemployment in the depression years. When one meets these men, they appear to be just like other people; but as one gets into talk with them, one sees that they are not. A man is marked, in one way or another, by years as a prisoner of war, or in hospital during a long illness, or in exile from his homeland. Similarly, a man is marked by years on the dole.

This is what I mean when I say that unemployment is an evil. And I am deeply concerned by the time during which we have tolerated it. I remind the reader that Merthyr – and many other places in South Wales, Tyneside, Scotland, Northern Ireland – has never had real full employment; some men and women, able and willing to work, were always unemployed even in the complacent 1950s and 1960s. Since the 'shake-out' of 1966, the national unemployment total has rarely gone below 500,000, and this has implied a much higher percentage rate in such areas. Since the autumn of 1970, the figure has stood at 800,000 or more, although the adverse balance of payments – the original reason for the squeeze – has become a big surplus. There is a real danger that we may congratulate ourselves on getting back to 'only' 500,000, that we may abandon the conception of full employment. Satisfaction comes easily, when problems are seen in abstract statistical terms. The Baldwin Government won an election in 1935 by bringing down unemployment from three million to 'only' a million and a half.

It may be realistic to say that no improvement can be expected until next autumn; but the calm statement of the fact is nevertheless an outrage. One day without work – the boredom and the emptiness of the slowly passing hours – is an ordeal. A week is worse; a month is worse still. If we are to acquire the necessary sense of the intolerable, we must stop watching the figures and imagine men and women living through those weeks and months.

2

Jack Saunders is sixty-one years old and has been unemployed since he was fifty-eight. This question of age is
one of the most saddening aspects of unemployment. In
good times and in booming towns, you can easily find men
still at work in their seventies. Being in good health, they
choose to keep busy rather than retire; often they leave
their former jobs and take on something lighter. In Merthyr,
a man of Saunders's age who leaves his job has little chance
of finding another. In most cases, obviously, he didn't leave
the job – it left him.

Like Gerry Donovan the Mayor, and Mr Zanelli who
keeps the café in the High Street, Jack Saunders speaks with
the purest of Welsh accents. To look at, judging by features
and colouring, he could be an Indian. That guess would be
wrong, for the Saunders family hails from Barbados in the
West Indies, and ultimately from Africa. Jack's grandfather,
who must have been a remarkable man, began life as a
slave and ended as a Baptist minister in Bristol. The next
Saunders moved to Cardiff, married a Welsh girl, and became an engine-driver on the Taff Vale Railway. The present
Mrs Saunders is Welsh too.

Though it seems hard to imagine nowadays, there was a
time when railwaymen were the aristocrats of labour. They
earned as much as miners or more, and they had security
even when business as a whole was in a poor way. Keeping
the trains running – safely, punctually, and faster than
any other known means of transport – was a matter of
great pride. The engine-driver at the controls of his mighty
locomotive was a hero to children, and of course more particularly to his own children. Admiration still rings in Jack

Saunders's voice when he shows off yellowing photographs of his father.

'I've got railway blood,' he says. Despite the depression, he was able to get work with the Great Western, which had taken over the Taff Vale and other lines. During the war he was in uniform, but still a railwayman; there was a section of the Royal Army Service Corps responsible for supervising the Egyptian railways and getting supplies up from the docks at Suez to the Eighth Army, unloading at El Alamein within range of enemy guns. One has to wonder what the Egyptian railwaymen thought of their instructor with the British uniform, Welsh accent, and pigmentation like their own.

Saunders came back to Merthyr (it had been his home since childhood, though he was born in Cardiff) and to an old stone-built house in Tramroadside North, the street alongside the tracks. His inclination was toward maintenance work, not the footplate; pride for him rested in the responsibility of keeping those thirty engines in the Merthyr sheds ready for service. He worked his way up to the position of chargeman, the railway word for maintenance foreman. His son had railway blood too, and started in the same line of work.

But, even in Saunders's young days, road transport had begun to take freight traffic away from the railways. The companies were shouting for subsidies in the 1930s, by the end of the war, they had ceased to be either profitable or efficient and waited resignedly for nationalisation. It was the Great Western, whose standards had always been the highest, that managed better than any of the other companies to maintain its traditions. 'It was a wonderful railway,' Saunders says fervently. Although he doubtless believes in 'the common ownership of the means of production, distribution and exchange' as much as anyone in Merthyr, he is also quite positive that the GWR has been going to pot ever since it became the Western Region of British Rail. A couple of years ago, he visited relatives at

Stroud and took five hours to get back. All the connections were late, the buffet at Gloucester had been closed, the waiting-room was locked, and nobody seemed to care. For a veteran of the Great Western, it was a deeply shocking experience.

In 1968, as a consequence of the ravages of the Beeching Plan, both Saunders and his son were made redundant. He showed me the letter that he received from an official in Cardiff. It reads: 'I am sorry that it is necessary to terminate your services, and I have pleasure in enclosing your Valedictory Certificate.' This is a document in copperplate script, suitable for hanging on the wall, and couched in these amiable terms: 'On the occasion of your retirement, Western Region Board of British Rail desire to congratulate you on the completion of 30 years' employment and wish you health and happiness in your retirement.' Saunders kept it, but had no inclination to hang it on the wall. He is a gentle man, but he is bitter about that word 'retirement'.

His son found work at Hoover's, and is still there. And at first, it looked as though Jack Saunders had evaded unemployment. There is a small pie factory – I mean, a small factory making pies – near Tramroadside North, and he was taken on as a foreman. It was undignified work after being in charge of railway engines, but it had a certain status and responsibility, and it was a wage.

After he had been at the factory for five months, a crate of pies fell off a loading-ramp. Saunders tried to stop it and broke a bone in his thumb. The bone healed slowly, so he was under the doctor's care longer than he expected. By the time he was fit again, his job had been filled. He received £21 as compensation. There was no trade union in the factory (though there is now) and although he'd chalked up thirty years' membership in the National Union of Railwaymen, the case was naturally not its affair.

He registered at the Employment Exchange, stating his qualifications, but they have never been able to find anything for him. He wrote letters, went through interviews, and stood at factory gates – without any result. Gradually, he gave up. Something might yet come along, he says, but fretting about it only makes you miserable. He expects to be one of the unemployed until, in the eyes of the Social Security office, his retirement is actually reached.

After 'retiring' from the railway, Saunders was entitled to a small pension from British Rail and a larger one under the old GWR scheme (which, he points out, was non-contributory). He commuted the pensions into a lump sum which, together with his redundancy payment, amounted to £458. When he had been unemployed for a year, the houses in Tramroadside North were demolished and he was given a new Council house. The rooms are a good deal larger than in the old house, and the Saunders' felt morally obliged to fit them out with new furniture, good carpets, and modern wallpaper. This took a big bite out of their capital.

Unemployment benefit (still known as the dole by most of those who get it) is at present £6 for a single man, or £9.70 for a man and wife. Additional benefit for children, including the family allowance, works out at £1.85 per child. The dole runs out after eighteen months, and the unemployed are then dependent on supplementary benefit (still known, generally, as national assistance). Even before that, many thousands of the unemployed get some supplementary benefit on top of the dole. In Merthyr, it's usually the rent – quite large in modern housing – that creates an entitlement; a Council tenant gets SB, an owner-occupier doesn't and their spending money is the same. Relations between Social Security officials and the unemployed are much better in Merthyr than in the big cities, or so I've been told by both. One hears little, on the one hand, of falsified claims and 'scrounging'; or, on the other hand, of people reluctant to claim; or of callous treatment and insulting investigations in the harsh tradition of the means test.

All this doesn't imply that the unemployed get enough money to pay for more than what, in the context of Britain in 1971, can fairly be regarded as necessities. Jack Saunders and his wife get £12.90 a week from the Social Security office. The rent is £3.72. Coal has gone up by 10p a bag to 82p, and they find that a bag a fortnight isn't enough in cold weather, but can't afford a fresh one before the fortnight is up. This 41p a week on coal is additional to 50p on electricity and 40p on gas. They pay 85p a week into a club on which they can draw for purchases of clothing. These fixed outgoings leave £7.02 for food and anything that one might describe as luxuries. In practice there are two luxuries. Though Saunders doesn't drink, he smokes – twenty cigarettes a day throughout his working life, ten a day now. And the television rental is 50p a week. A friend arranged it through some sort of scheme, but this will run out in 1972 and, so far as they can see, they'll have to give up the set. Expenditure on outside entertainment is zero; holidays, zero; travel, zero. On the rare occasions when Saunders goes away, he uses his free railway pass.

Apart from his marriage and his home, Saunders's life centres on three things. He is deeply religious, he is devoted to music, and he keeps in touch with old railway workmates. An old upright piano, the principal relic of Tramroadside North, stands in the living-room; he plays by the hour, though the damaged thumb is a handicap, as it is in gardening. On Saturday evenings, he sometimes has a few neighbours in for a singsong. Once a week, he delivers the parish magazine in the district. And on Thursday afternoons, he goes down to the Railway Club. 'We all feel it's broken our hearts, what's been done to the railways', he says; these reunions must be melancholy occasions.

Four years from now, Jack Saunders will be sixty-five. One can imagine him retiring (in the genuine sense) at that age and being content with his home and his piano. Some may feel that his leaving the working world seven years early doesn't matter much. It matters to him. In the material sense, what matters is being reduced to a pensioner's standard of living seven years before he had reckoned with it. Seven years are seven years, after all. Far more than that, what matters is the sense of being expelled, of being turned out of his rightful place, while he was still carrying out his duties responsibly and well. He takes that hard.

3

Bill Corcoran is another of those Welsh Irishmen, or Irish Welshmen; it was his great-grandfather who came from Ireland, he thinks. He is unemployed at forty-two, and feels that he has years of good work still in him. The question is whether they will be spent in Merthyr. You notice a certain difference about this – a difference of mood rather than opinion – between him and his wife, Iris. He dislikes too much upheaval; she, a vivacious lightweight blonde, inclines toward new experiences. She enjoys trips to London and wouldn't mind living there. He would be unhappy about leaving Merthyr. The Corcorans, all bright at school and all qualified for good jobs, have scattered; there is a brother in Cardiff, a brother in London, a brother and a sister in the north of England. It would be a pity if Merthyr had no place for any Corcorans at all.

Bill Corcoran grew up with his father, a miner, on the dole for five years. Iris's father was a miner too. With this background, they have always lived rather frugally and saved money. They own an oldish terrace house near the centre of town. There is little snobbery or keeping up with the Joneses in Merthyr; but in most places, one would be surprised to find a manager in a large factory, with a salary of £2,550, living in this kind of house. Corcoran says he's always had a feeling that you never know what might happen. As events proved, he was quite right.

The end of the war, as I have mentioned, was an uneasy period for Merthyr, and it seemed possible that mass unemployment was coming back. Corcoran stayed on at school to the age of seventeen; he is glad of it in retrospect, but his main reason was that there were no jobs going. Then

Teddington Aircraft Controls arrived, and he was taken on for a five-year apprenticeship. He has worked as both engineer and draughtsman, and studied to become a graduate of the Institute of Mechanical Engineering. Eventually he rose to the status of manager, and was in charge of a number of special projects. This involved him in travelling for consultation with other firms – to various parts of Britain, to France, and twice to America. For a time, he also taught at the College of Further Education, but he had to give this up because of the travelling.

Corcoran is one of those people who are convinced – and he ought to know – that TAC could have kept going if all its projects had been vigorously pursued. When prospects in the aircraft industry got disappointing, there was a lot of talk about diversification, and Corcoran's particular responsibility was the development of a kidney machine. He enjoyed working out the requirements with doctors in leading hospitals and finding common ground with engineers in the French firm which was to join in the development. But he always had a feeling that the management wasn't really behind the idea. He is sure that it was perfectly feasible, but it came to nothing.

When TAC closed down, he was offered a job in Streatham (where, it will be remembered, the work was to be continued). He devoted his fortnight's summer holiday to investigating the possibilities. The Corcorans have always taken caravan holidays, so they were happy to spend the fortnight at the Crystal Palace caravan site. Corcoran didn't believe that the job at Streatham would be safe; on the other hand, what he saw of the engineering industry in the outskirts of London gave him confidence that there would be other jobs, in case of need, for a man with his qualifications. After much family discussion, the Corcorans decided to accept the Streatham opening.

No sooner had they returned to Merthyr than they discovered that the opening was now closed. The work was going to Yeovil, in the hands of Normalair Garrett. Corcoran embarked on another reconnaissance and spent a weekend at Yeovil. This, he quickly saw, was quite a different proposition. If anything happened to his job, he would be left high and dry; there is practically nothing else around Yeovil, except farming. A house at Yeovil would cost him much more than he could get for his Merthyr home, and no help in the way of a low-interest loan was offered by Normalair Garrett. It wasn't at all out of the question that he could find himself saddled with a mortgage and unemployed in a rural area. Moreover, the Corcorans have a girl of thirteen and a boy of six, and continual moving can be harmful to education.

He asked Normalair Garrett to give him a guarantee of three years' employment. The point of making it three years, principally, was that this would take Teresa as far as O-levels. The company replied that it could give no guarantee at all. Clearly, Yeovil was too much of a risk. That left Corcoran working out his notice and signing on at the Employment Exchange.

It's a peculiar feeling, he says, to wake up in the morning and realize that he has nowhere to go. It's peculiar to be still at home after the children have gone to school. But there are jobs to do about the house which he hasn't had time for before, so he hasn't begun to feel at a loose end. Nor has his standard of living gone down; he never lived up to his salary, and he is on earnings-related benefit, which continues for six months before the drop to basic unemployment scales. There is no depression in the house, nor is there self-pity. Among the unemployed, a great many people are worse off.

Still, a man is bound to wonder how long it will last. Corcoran has applied for six jobs, without success. He doesn't expect to strike lucky in Merthyr. When I met him, he was waiting for a reply from a firm in Abergavenny, nineteen miles away. He has a car, but the journey will be no fun when there's snow on the Heads of the Valleys Road (maximum height 1,350 feet).

If no job turns up, he has another idea. He could become the tenant of a garage, and he has written to Texaco about this. The garage might not be in Merthyr or in the nearby valleys, which are short on garages. It might mean a move, and then the problem of security and Teresa's O-levels would arise again. However, if the idea does work out it will be a solution of a kind, and it will reduce the unemployment total by one.

Whether this would be a good bargain for the nation, considering the work that Bill Corcoran is capable of doing, is another matter.

4

Every morning, Betty Harrington leaves home before eight o'clock. She walks down the precipitous streets from Park Crescent, which is on a hill above Merthyr, and catches the bus for the thirteen-mile journey to Pontypridd, where she works in the Electricity Board's saleroom. The Board has promised to transfer her to Merthyr as soon as possible. This is not exactly her career, nor her choice; she hasn't worked since she was married. But Joe Harrington is un-unemployed.

It is Joe Harrington, therefore, who gives the two girls their breakfast and gets them off to school. Then he does the housework and the shopping, and makes lunch for himself and the girls; the Harringtons consider school dinners a poor bargain. He takes rather a long time over the domestic chores, not being the kind of man whose tastes and talents lie in that direction. The situation is one that has become increasingly common as unemployment has spread. Harrington, a man of radical views, might not mind if it were a matter of women's lib; unemployment is something else.

Given the family background, one could hardly expect him to be an exponent of the virtues of free enterprise. His father worked in the pits from boyhood, was gassed in the 1914-18 war, signed on as a regular, became a staff-sergeant in the Indian Army, returned to unemployment in Merthyr, put in a spell as a labourer in London, and was on the dole from 1928 to 1939 – except when he was fighting in Spain with the International Brigade. In the Second World War he found factory work, but he ended up as a Merthyr Council labourer. The middle-class public, I sometimes feel, might have a different view of the world if the memoirs serialized in Sunday papers weren't always by diplomats or generals.

Since the mining industry went into decline, 'don't go down the pit' has been the advice given by many an old miner to his sons. Of two brothers, Illtyd Harrington became a teacher in London and Joe a clerical worker. His first employer was a fruit wholesaler in Merthyr; his second was the Murphy radio factory at Hirwaun, which made him redundant in 1952. Then he was an insurance agent, and eventually joined Teddington Aircraft Controls, where he worked in the drawing office. He was chairman of the Clerical and Administrative Workers' Union branch, and a member of the Action Committee which was formed in an effort to save the TAC factory or get another company to take over. Thanks to this activity, he is a well-known figure in Merthyr, and when I tried to get the background facts about the TAC collapse I was told on all sides that I ought to talk to Joe Harrington. This, naturally, doesn't prevent him from being one of the unemployed.

In that capacity, he is under several disadvantages. In the first place, he never earned more than £23 a week, so his earnings-related benefit – for the family of four – comes to only £16.60. That should amply explain why Mrs Harrington is at work.

Secondly, it is harder to find office work around Merthyr than any other kind. Harrington has applied wherever there is the hint or rumour of a chance; the answer is invariably 'We'll let you know'.

Thirdly – and this is of key importance to an understanding of life on the dole – the chances of finding work are directly related to a man's financial resources. Unto him who hath, on the whole, shall be given. This applies particularly to the question of mobility. A house in Merthyr can be sold, at the most, for £4,000. A house in the London area or the Midlands, or in a town like Yeovil, can be found for about £7,000. For a man like Bill Corcoran, with enough in the bank for a down payment and a salary scale that would impress a mortgage company favourably, this is a feasible proposition; it is job security, as we have seen, that is the stumbling-block. For a man like Joe Harrington, the transaction is beyond his reach in any case.

The factor is significant, too, with regard to jobs that involve a daily journey. Harrington has no car. The place where he would be most likely to find an office job is, obviously, Cardiff; but the price of a season ticket works out at £2.40 a week. After knocking that off his net earnings, he might not be much better off than he is unemployed. If he found work in another of the valleys – in Rhymney or Ebbw Vale – he would be let in for bus fares that seem to go up once a year. Besides, the services are so bad – with long shivering waits where you have to change – that he would see hardly anything of his children.

Joe Harrington, too, is not despondent. But when he talks about his position and prospects, you catch the overtones of something that often goes with unemployment: the sense of being boxed in, the feeling that any possible solution has its nullifying catch. Far away from Merthyr, it is sometimes said – it was said even in the 1930s – that the unemployed ought to do more to help themselves. One would like to know exactly what Joe Harrington is supposed to do.

5

From about the middle of 1971, the unemployment figures in South Wales began to rise significantly in the younger age-groups: youth unemployment as officially defined (age 15 to 18) and the first category of adult unemployment (age 18 to 21). This trend is doubly disturbing. It is clear evidence of a stagnant and gloomy economic situation, for an employer who doesn't want to take on and train young workers obviously hasn't much faith in the future. And it can leave a community landed with a group of young people who, failing to acquire a trade or settle in a secure job, become resigned to spells in and out of work, to drifting through life, to the bitter knowledge that they have missed the vital chance. The hallmark of an unhealthy society – in Northern Ireland, say, or in the black ghettoes of American cities – is always a high rate of youth unemployment.

In Merthyr, there are two types of young people without work. There are those who leave school with GCEs or other qualifications and don't find the openings for which they had hoped. Some take inferior jobs rather than do nothing, some leave Merthyr, and some occupy their time by signing on for further education courses which they didn't really want to take (these form a group of 'disguised' unemployed and don't appear in the statistics). For these reasons, there are fewer unemployed young people of this type than one might expect – which does not mean that everything is all right for those concerned. It is all the more depressing that the ranks of the unemployed do include more young people with good qualifications than ever before.

The other type is the youngster who just wants a job. He

is in one of the lower streams at the comprehensive, he doesn't take GCE, he leaves school at fifteen. Not being choosy, he finds work fairly easily in prosperous times; but if conditions are bad, he is in the weakest possible position. Because of the excellence of the schools, there are not so many young people of this type in Merthyr as in many British towns. But it goes without saying that there are some, and the outlook for them has never – at least, never since the 'thirties – been so discouraging as it is now.

Daniel Keating is eighteen, which means that he has graduated from the Careers Office to the Employment Exchange where the men go. He is a good-looking youngster, his face framed by fair hair worn long in the style of the 1970s. He is slightly built and doesn't strike you as muscular; his complexion is very clear and his skin looks delicate, a fact whose relevance will become evident as we follow his brief career. He talks quietly and rather defensively. Life has not been encouraging for him.

The Keatings are Catholics, and Daniel is the fourth of five children. Three are working and two unemployed, making a 40% unemployment rate for the present Keating generation. Their father is drawing the old age pension. There has never been any money to spare in the family; they live in one of the old stone houses, due to be demolished within the next year or two.

On leaving school, Daniel got a job in a fishmonger's shop at £7 a week and kept it for about a year. Then he heard that a coal merchant, for whom his eldest brother was working, had a vacancy. By making a move, he was able to raise his earnings to £12 a week and also to acquire a skill, for he was trained to drive a fork-lift truck. He was contented in this job, and stayed for nearly two years.

But he found that he was getting a rash on his hands. The doctor couldn't do much about it. He went sick and took time off work; the rash disappeared. When he returned to work, the rash appeared again. He drew the conclusion that coal-dust was bad for his skin. Reluctantly, he gave up the job.

Daniel and his twenty-three-year-old brother share a bedroom in the old house. The brother, who used to be a bricklayer's mate, has been unemployed for four months; Daniel has now been out of work for six. Every day, they buy the *South Wales Echo* as soon as it's on sale and study the advertisements. Then they go job-hunting. They compare their experiences when they come in for supper. So far, they have both been unlucky.

There isn't a factory in Merthyr and the surrounding villages where Daniel hasn't applied for work. He has even made a trip to Swansea, where a friend from school found a job, but the bus fare was spent in vain. The only real chance, he thinks, is on the building sites. You have to find out where a new contract is being started and get there at the right moment. But in winter the builders lay off men, and it's pointless to apply.

I asked him whether he couldn't go back to the fishmonger's. He had 'given satisfaction' there, as the phrase goes. Daniel explained that this was a school-leaver's job. In fact, at quite a number of the places where he has applied for work, he is told that the employer is looking for 'a young lad' – at corresponding wages, naturally. When there is unemployment, it is possible to be too old at eighteen.

'I don't mind what I do,' Daniel says. 'Up at the Exchange, they ask you what sort of job you're looking for. I'm just looking. Any job at all, I'll try it. I'll go anywhere, if I can find work.'

Merthyr, apparently, has nothing to offer to Daniel Keating. Perhaps in London or in the major industrial areas, there might be a niche. But since it's a matter of looking for labouring work, the Irish and the Commonwealth immigrants are there already; and the promised land is nowhere, with the national unemployment total on the million mark. One needs some optimism, anyway, to launch oneself into the unknown without friends on the spot, without a place to live, without money. Optimism is what Daniel no longer possesses.

Among the unemployed people with whom I talked in Merthyr, several were moderately confident that their luck would turn up in a matter of weeks, or months at the worst. Daniel Keating was not hopeful at all. Defeat and rejection had become the norm for him. And of all those I met, he is the youngest.

6

The staff of any Employment Exchange, when talking candidly, will say that some unemployed men and women give the impression that they don't expect to get a job, and wouldn't do it properly if they did get it. 'Unlikely to impress an employer favourably' is the usual phrase. If the verdict is sometimes unjust, there are instances when it is a fair comment.

No such description could apply to Mrs Isabel Chivers. 'Why the hell are you unemployed?' is what I wanted to say to her. Picture a lively, cheerful woman, obviously intelligent, good at expressing herself clearly, full of energy, with a ready sense of humour – and pretty too, which helps in this world. Meeting her socially, one would identify her as the valued secretary of a senior executive. This guess would be correct. Unfortunately, the senior executive was at Teddington Aircraft Controls.

Mr Bernard Chivers also worked at TAC, so the collapse caused something of a family crisis. He has been able to find work at Hoover's. This is not ideal, for several reasons. The Chivers live at Trefechan, up on the edge of the Brecon Beacons, which is much farther from Hoover's than from the Teddington factory. The new job is less skilled and less interesting than the old one. And Chivers is on night work for alternate fortnights, to the annoyance of his wife who likes going out with him in the evenings. Still, he considers himself lucky. He knows a precision-lathe engineer who is sweeping the floor at Hoover's – not to mention plenty who are still on the dole.

'I'm still in the right age bracket,' he says rather sharply. 'A man who was fifty when it happened – he's in trouble.'

Both the Chivers are older than they look, and turn out surprisingly to have a son of nineteen as well as one of thirteen. The elder boy is in his first year at Swansea University, studying mechanical engineering. In Wales today, this is not a guarantee of an expanding future. 'There's men with degrees digging ditches,' Bernard Chivers tells me. It's reasonable to suppose that the son, after he graduates, will be able to get a decent job in some other part of Britain. But when the discussion reaches this point, Mrs Chivers says indignantly: 'Why should they all have to leave, just because they get degrees? What's wrong with Wales?' The Chivers family is evidently a tightly-knit household, with no desire to be scattered.

As for Isabel Chivers, she is one of those women who enjoy working. She has worked all her life, except for two brief spells when each child was a baby. She doesn't criticize women who simply want to be housewives, but it's very clear that she is a different type. 'Oh, I get so bored, stuck in the house – and it's only been a few weeks!' she exclaims. The Council house isn't very large; a woman of Mrs Chivers's vigour could sweep and dust it in half an hour. On the quiet Trefechan estate, a car going along the road is something to notice. In winter, the days seem very long.

With the position she has had, and her references, Mrs Chivers could walk into another job in some parts of the country. In Merthyr, it's not so simple. She has had two interviews, but neither of them led to anything. On the afternoon when I met her, she had just come in from a third interview. 'They'll let me know – they've got other candidates to see,' she told me. She has high hopes of getting a job before long, but she expects that it will be less interesting and less responsible than the job at TAC.

She was earning £17.50 – an indication of the wage levels acceptable in Merthyr, at a time when 'temps' in London can easily take home £20. The double income, however, had placed the Chivers above the need to budget closely or hesitate over minor luxuries. Now, things are different. Mrs Chivers had been paying the 'married woman's stamp' instead of full National Insurance, so she is not entitled to unemployment benefit. So long as she is out of work, spending money is drastically reduced. It is indeed lucky that Bernard Chivers found a job at Hoover's.

When the monthly unemployment figures come out, newspapers sometimes stress the percentage of male unemployment as a particularly grave aspect of the situation. The implication seems to be that it is worse for men to be unemployed than for women. In Merthyr, working-class men of the older generation tend to fall in with this view; some, indeed, maintain that women ought to bow out of the labour market when men can't find jobs. The historical truth, however, is that the virtual absence of work for women in the 'thirties was a substantial cause of the poverty into which so many families descended when the men were unemployed. Conversely, the appearance of women's jobs in wartime and thereafter brought Merthyr as near to prosperity as it has ever come.

Isabel Chivers, at all events, is fully in the category of the unemployed, taking this term to define a person who is trained to work, anxious to work, and prevented from working. If she had wanted to be a housewife, she would have been one all along.

7

In Merthyr's demonstration against unemployment, the placard carried by a child and reading 'My Grandpa Wants Work' was obviously worth following up. I found that the grandpa, named Harry Jones, has no grey hairs and certainly doesn't consider himself beyond working age. Nor has he got beyond family responsibilities. He has two adult sons and a grand-daughter, but he also has a daughter of sixteen and a son of fourteen.

In the engineering industry, which now dominates Merthyr's economy, lifelong security is exceptional and workers are used to a certain amount of snakes and ladders. Jones is out of a job for the fourth time in his life. The first time was in the depression years, after he had completed an apprenticeship in the Great Western Railway's workshops at Swindon. The apprenticeship was obtained quite easily, since his father was an engine-driver, but it didn't guarantee a job; the company habitually trained more apprentices than it intended to employ. Young Jones was on the dole for over a year. There was no question of dire poverty, however, because his father was earning £5 a week – 'fabulous for Merthyr in those days,' Jones recalls. He had six shillings a week pocket-money and could take a girl out when he felt like it; this too was fabulous, or at least exceptional, for youngsters at the time.

The outlook in Merthyr looked bleak, so he migrated to the outskirts of London and found work in an engineering factory. Then, while he was at home for Christmas, he heard of a vacancy for a fitter in the railway sheds and snapped it up. He must have been a good fitter; he was kept out of uniform as an essential worker during the war, and stayed in the job until 1952. Then he moved to Teddington Aircraft Controls.

In 1961, the project on which Jones was working was transferred to a development unit at Pontardulais, thirty-five miles from Merthyr. By this time he had bought a house and sunk some money in modernizing it; besides, the children were at various stages of their education. Moving to Pontardulais wasn't an attractive prospect. He gave up the job.

His next employer was Hoover. This was the peak of his career if one judges by status; he became a quality controller. But in 1965 the company had to cut down its labour force, and invited each grade to offer candidates for 'voluntary severance'. The feeling among the quality controllers favoured the old principle of 'last in first out', and Jones had been at Hoover's for only four years. Once again, he was unemployed.

Without much of a gap, he was able to find a job in the toolroom of Cold Precision Forgings. This firm had recently arrived at Merthyr's industrial estate, and was in a good way of business making metal parts for the motor industry. Now over fifty, Jones congratulated himself on getting settled for the rest of his working life. It was a bad jolt for him when, in 1970, the company decided to clear out of Merthyr.

The redundancy payment laid down by law amounted to £150 – not a huge sum, because Jones had been at CPF for only five years. He was offered another £180 to stay on for the six months that the firm needed to complete its contracts, and to help in the run-down. This looked like a silver lining to the cloud, and he accepted. Seen in retrospect, it may have been the wrong decision. By April 1971, when Jones drew his last pay-packet, the economic situation was worse than before and another major employer in Merthyr – TAC – was preparing to close down.

When I met him, Harry Jones had been unemployed for seven months. Nothing of the kind had happened to him since boyhood. He had written so many applications that postage was an item in the family budget, and been given seven interviews. Every employer had been impressed with his qualifications and experience. On one occasion, he was practically given the job, with the proviso that there was one other candidate still to be interviewed. The other man got the job; Jones knows who he is, and the difference is ten years in age. 'You can't blame them,' he said to me resignedly. In the search for a job in Merthyr – except, perhaps, as Member of Parliament – being over fifty is a grave handicap. Jones now wonders if he'll get a job as an engineer at all, and is thinking of a position with Securicor, which has proved a haven for some of the redundant. But Securicor too may have its age limits.

At CPF, with a bonus and three evenings of overtime, Jones could take home £28.30 a week. In Merthyr, this is in the upper bracket. As an unemployed man, he drew £18 in earnings-related benefit plus £1.50 from the union. Both of these finished after six months, and now he is down to £15.75 from the Social Security office. The redundancy money went straight into the bank and has stayed there; some working-class people, just as much as any rentier, have a prudent aversion to 'biting into capital'. There was no question of a holiday in 1971. Jones is determined to live on what comes in every week so long as it's necessary. Since this is only slightly more than half his earnings at CPF, the cut in spending is considerable. But if you have a boy and a girl in their teens, they have to leave the house on a solid breakfast and decently dressed. The cut must come somewhere else.

For years, Harry Jones has been spending Friday and Saturday evenings at a club where he plays snooker. He is devoted to the game and a valued member of the club team. Two friends of his are also regular players, and their sessions have become an invariable custom. It isn't natural to play snooker without a drink handy, and it certainly isn't proper to fail to stand your round. The friends are both still in work, and they refuse to let Jones take his turn. He accepts a pint, makes it last, and declares that he doesn't feel like any more. Since he used to spend five pounds or so in the course of the two evenings, this abstinence isn't very convincing. There was an understanding that he would put the score right when he found a job, but after seven months this is wearing rather thin. The situation is becoming more and more awkward. He can see the time coming when he will have to give up snooker, which would be like asking a real enthusiast to give up bridge or chess. There are worse tragedies in the world; people in India are starving; and indeed Harry Jones talks about his deprivation with a wry smile. But deprivation has to be seen in terms of what a man has grown used to, and of what is customary in a community. Through the smile, it's easy to see that the sense of humiliation is real.

An important financial problem is keeping the car on the road. It is a 1964 model and Jones had been thinking of replacing it, but of course that's out of the question since he lost his job. The car does hardly any mileage; when in work, he didn't hesitate before taking the family to the coast or the mountains on a fine day, but now the cost of a gallon of petrol is a matter for careful consideration. The reason for keeping the car is that he could accept a job at a distance from Merthyr. There was a prospect, for instance, at Cardiff airport, although in the end the airport shelved its expansion plans and the prospect vanished. Jones was just going off earnings-related benefit when he had to renew the licence for the car and buy some essential new parts. The calculations were difficult.

When one thinks about unemployment as a human experience, one is led naturally to the question: what do the unemployed do with their time? After all, they are people whose lives have been dominated by work, people for whom a long stretch of leisure is unnatural. It seemed to me that they dealt with the problem, on the whole, much better than one might expect. Of course, looking for work – writing letters, waiting for interviews, chasing possibilities and rumours – is something of an occupation. Then, the unemployed spend quite a lot of time talking (especially if they are Welsh); the routine of signing on and drawing dole once a week has become quite a social occasion, and when I went to the Employment Exchange I noticed that many people arrived early and were in no hurry to go home. Those who are active in political organizations or in the Churches, as one would suppose, put in a good deal of voluntary work. Those who enjoy reading read; those who can play a musical instrument play it.

But the resource that's most often mentioned is 'doing jobs about the house'. Many of the unemployed in Merthyr own their houses, so any improvement is all to the good. A building job is a durable achievement, unlike washing the dishes or sweeping the floor; and, since it could be done by a man who's paid for it, it is the best possible imitation of actually having work. Above all, it creates a routine. You start at a fixed time in the morning, you take an hour off for lunch, you finish up pleasantly tired and hungry when the time comes to put away your tools and change out of your overalls – just as if you were at the factory.

Harry Jones has pretty well transformed his old house in Alma Street. Some years ago, a new bathroom and kitchen were built on at the back; this was done by a builder and cost over £1,000, of which £250 came from an improvement grant. Later, Jones decided to remove a wall and turn the two small downstairs rooms into one larger room. He did this himself at the weekends, but he wasn't satisfied with the finish, and when he became unemployed he got it just as he wanted it. Then he put down an even concrete floor throughout; the front room had been floored with old tiles and the back room with wood, and the height had been slightly different. After this, he enlarged the window facing the street. Of course, he has gone over all the inside walls carefully, repairing the plaster and putting up new wallpaper.

E

There comes a time, however, when there's nothing more to do, unless you make the absurd decision to undo what you've just done. Besides, even do-it-yourself building work costs money in materials. For the unemployed, 'jobs about the house' can be no more than a finite resource. Harry Jones has almost reached the limits.

This is the danger point. I noticed – clearly, the observation wasn't surprising – that the degree to which an unemployed man finds life empty can be related with some exactitude to the number of weeks or months since he stopped working. A man who had lost his job a couple of weeks ago would answer my questions briefly and then see me to the door, very much as a man with a job would do if, for instance, an interviewer from an opinion poll came to the house. But a man who had been on the dole for months would keep me chatting of this and that, telling irrelevant stories or bringing up childhood memories, in an understandable desire to hang on to my company – anyone's company – and fend off the return to vacant time.

Harry Jones is a long way from the human deterioration that can await the long-term unemployed, and he doesn't strike one as the kind of man who would ever fall into it. He is a man with pride and self-control, very conscious of being a skilled engineer, on the alert for a hint of a chance to find work. But he is getting very bored and frustrated, and nothing is happening to make him more hopeful. Seven months out of work is a long time. The unemployment situation is getting worse, and Harry Jones is getting older.

He is also a man of imagination. Thinking things over – and he has plenty of time to do that – he can envisage what has to be endured by a man who is on the dole for a year, a year and a half . . . who knows?

After a minute of thoughtful silence, he looked directly at me and said: 'I don't know what kind of a feeling I'll get, if this goes on.'

8

Ever since Freda Smart left school, she has been the breadwinner of the family. Her father, who was a miner, died when he was quite young. Her sister suffered from spinabifida and was never able to walk. Her mother stayed at home, looking after the invalid. Freda went out to work. Eventually the girl with spinabifida died, but by that time the mother was on the old age pension.

For one reason or another – perhaps because she had two dependants – Freda Smart has not married. Her home for most of her life was an old cottage in a tangle of streets near the Taf – a tangle that has been cleared away, to be replaced by flats which look rather too big for their surroundings. The Smarts, mother and daughter, now live in a Council house on the distinctly shabby estate along the road to Swansea. They feel isolated there, remote from old neighbours and from the life of the town.

Miss Smart's job was at Teddington Aircraft Controls, as a packer in the despatching department. After sixteen years, her basic wage was still only £12 a week, with earnings that usually came to £16 thanks to overtime. However, she was perfectly happy. She is a person – or so I felt when I talked to her – who is easily satisfied. She liked her immediate boss and all the other workers in the department. Clearly, the factory provided a secure and friendly environment: provided, indeed, most of what we understand by social life. 'The atmosphere was lovely – everybody was so happy,' she told me. Looking back, she declares fervently: 'I loved every minute of it.'

Moreover, in Miss Smart's view TAC was a wonderful factory. The skilled engineers have stories to tell of faulty planning and frustrated efforts, but all this passed over her head. There was always plenty to do, so far as she was concerned. 'It was a treat going in there every morning,' she says. What impressed her most was that the place was kept beautifully clean. 'They washed the floors so regular, you'd never think it was a factory.'

She never took time off; it worried her to think of the department being short. On one occasion, she did have to go into hospital for a minor operation. But, as she wasn't due at the hospital until the afternoon, she worked in the morning.

At home, Mrs Smart was not entirely alone. There is a dog (actually, a bitch) who is very much one of the family. Miss Smart, however, always came home to lunch. It is quite a long way from the Swansea Road estate to the factory; fortunately she knew an engineer who also lived on the estate, also came home for lunch, and had a car. So she had a lift, twice a day in each direction. This was one more example of the happy, friendly atmosphere.

Of all the workers at TAC, no one can have been more grieved than Miss Smart by the news that the factory was to close down. She was told that she could stay until the very end; presumably packers were needed until there was absolutely nothing to pack. But the gradual run-down was saddening. The quiet after most of the machines had stopped working was uncanny. There was less and less work in the despatching department, so Miss Smart used to take her knitting.

Her boss left to start a small business in Cornwall. 'It's awful to see good men going away,' Miss Smart comments. Other men and women whom she knew left as one batch of redundancies followed another. She knows what has happened to each of them – those who are at Hoover's, those who are travelling to work at Treforest or Pontypridd, those who haven't found anything. It was awkward when the man who gave her the lifts was dismissed. She had to walk across the estate to the bus-stop, and then quite a distance the other end. But she continued to come home for lunch. By that time, it was only for another four weeks.

So the last day came: Friday, 12 November 1971. The factory is deserted, and no one knows whether the clean, spacious workshops have any future. The fine autumn weather turns to winter, always chilling on the wind-swept Swansea Road estate.

'I can't just sit at home,' Miss Smart told me. 'I love my home, mind, but I can't sit here all day, I really can't. I've always gone out to work, you see. I'm only happy when I've got something to do. I like walking, out with the dog. But she's getting old now, you can't take her far.'

'I suppose you're looking for something else,' I said.

'Well, it seems funny, but I can't bring myself to do anything about it. Anywhere else would be so different after Teddington's, wouldn't it? I don't think I fancy working in another factory. Teddington's was such a lovely place, I wouldn't be happy in just any old factory. A shop would be better, I think. I believe that's what I'll do, I'll look for a job in one of the shops.'

They do have vacancies in the shops, sometimes.

9

Cherry Grove, just as one would imagine from its name, is a quiet side-street in a modern housing estate. The familiar Borough Council architecture, the concrete roadway, the strip of grass and the young trees planted at regular intervals are exactly what one sees in similar streets anywhere from Dover to Carlisle. Only after entering a house on the right-hand side (going from Gurnos Road) and going into the back room does one catch another of those spectacular views and, with it, the feel of Merthyr Tydfil.

Moreover, nothing in the Hiers' house is different from the Cherry Grove norm. There is the three-piece suite, probably from the Co-op's furnishing department, the television set, the picture over the fireplace. The rooms have been papered not long ago – in the Hier family, as it happens, it's Mother who is the handy one. The house is crowded at times, as there are five children, but everything is kept firmly in its place. The kettle, at suitable times, is on for tea. One has to talk to the Hiers to know that theirs isn't and never has been the world of working-class 'affluence' – of polishing the new car and holidays in Majorca. One has to be told, in particular, that unemployment dominates this home like a mysterious congenital disease.

Idris Hier, now forty-eight years old, recalls a childhood marked by the worst of the old poverty. His father, a miner forced out of the pits by pneumoconiosis, died in 1932. Somehow, or other, Idris Hier didn't find his way into a skilled trade. On the employment register, he appeared as 'labourer'. After he married, he started working in a scrapyard belonging to his brother-in-law. It was a small business, with only four on the payroll. Hier, who has trouble with his chest, wasn't required to exert himself too much. The wages wouldn't have met with the approval of a trade union, but the scrapyard made only enough to keep ticking over, and one can't make demands on one's brother-in-law. It was a friendly place, and Hier felt that he had his niche in the world. He worked there for eighteen years.

But scrap can be quite big business. When an efficient firm of contractors, working with container lorries, appeared on the scene, the family scrapyard was doomed. Four years ago, it closed down. Idris Hier has been out of work ever since. With no particular qualifications, and with his weak chest which rules out heavy work, he is one of those men described at the Employment Exchange as 'difficult to place'. I got the impression that he is resigned to unemployment. The deepening gloom over Merthyr makes this resignation appear perfectly rational.

'Things are getting worse, aren't they?' he says. 'Everybody knows that. Firms closing down all the time, and nothing starting up. I used to go round looking for a job, but what's the point now? It's only asking at the same places where I got nothing before.'

Leonard Hier will be nineteen while this book is in the press. When he left school, he saw himself – or so I should guess – as the one who would bring the family up to another level in the gradations of the working-class. He didn't take the first job that was to be found; he made plans. He took a course at the College of Further Education, and emerged in June 1971 qualified as a laboratory technician. But there are not many labs within reach of Merthyr, and it's safe to say that there are few or none expanding their work and looking for junior staff. Leonard Hier has not found a job.

Lynn Hier is seventeen. She too went to the College of Further Education, taking a course in office work. She failed the final exam in shorthand. 'I can write it, mind,' she explained to me with a smile, 'only I can't read what I've written, not all of it.' However, she passed as 'satisfactory' in typing and also in accounts; she is obviously a bright girl, and she would have got a job if she had completed her course in June 1970. June 1971 was different. She wrote ten letters of application as soon as she got her exam results, and ever since then she has tried for two or three jobs every week, but she hasn't been lucky yet. She types letters for the Rector two mornings a week (the Hiers are a church-going family). Lynn. who is a realist, says: 'He's only doing us a good turn, I know that.'

For those who are fond of statistics, the unemployment rate among insured workers in the Hier household is now 100%. It isn't an encouraging atmosphere for the three children who are still at school. Nor is it cheerful for the unemployed, as the weeks and months go by without a lucky break for any of the three. Human character is varied, however, even in the same family. Idris Hier, as I have said, is philosophical about the situation. Leonard is far more depressed; he sat gloomily slumped in his chair while I was in the house and didn't want to talk about himself. The setback to his hopes, clearly, has been painful. Most of what I have said about him, I gathered from his parents or from Lynn, who talks readily. She is a vivacious girl of considerable spirit, and her reaction to unemployment is indignation. 'It's stupid, all these people doing nothing, *stupid*!' she exclaims. The indignation combines with a defiant optimism; it can't go on for ever, she thinks, and one guesses that she keeps the family in good heart.

Lynn is a Merthyr patriot. She has no experience of the world, nor indeed of England, because the Hiers have never taken a holiday away from home. She has been to the Glamorgan coast for the day with friends who own a car, and that is all. She would like to travel, but not as an escape. 'There's people who've been all over the world, and they've come back to Merthyr,' she points out. Merthyr doesn't get a fair deal, in her view, because outsiders think it's a horrible place. 'Beautiful it is really – don't you think so?' Even if I didn't think so, I shouldn't have the heart to disagree.

As they are living at home, Leonard and Lynn get the

minimum of unemployment benefit. The family income, including family allowances for the younger children, totals £27.20. With seven mouths to feed, it is not a huge sum. One job, even at 'under 21' wages, could make a deal of difference.

One would very much like to look ahead a year or so and know what happens to the Hier family. Idris Hier might get a chance any day, through the neighbourly grapevine which is well developed in Merthyr, but after four years it can't – to say the least – be counted on. Lynn will keep up her energetic applications, but if she ends up as a shop assistant or doing assembly-line work in a factory, that office training will be wasted. Leonard can be imagined leaving Merthyr, when the strain of sitting about the house becomes intolerable. Or he might renounce his ambitions; when I saw him, he was wondering whether to ask for a job as a postman. Boys who left school when he did are postmen now and, when all is said and done, they are earning. Almost as much as lasting unemployment, this would be a defeat, and a defeat that would leave a deep sense of bitterness. It would be the end of his ambition to build a career, for second chances are rare. And the nation would be losing one more lab technician.

In the worst case, 100% unemployment in the Hier family might go on and on.

10

David Fuller is a large man with square shoulders, an almost monumental head, a broad face, and horn-rimmed spectacles resting like fixtures on his nose and ears. When he does anything – pours out tea, puts sugar in his cup, pulls out a chair and sits down – he does it with sureness and deliberation. A man, one guesses, confident of solving any problem that comes his way by taking it methodically and reflectively. Probably, also, a man who doesn't alter his ways without conscious decision; one notes that, after living for twenty-five years in Merthyr with a Welsh wife he still speaks with the unalloyed accent of his native London. When he has the right house, the right job, the right routine, he sticks to it. In fact, he worked for the same employer for thirty-seven years.

Fuller's birthplace was Feltham, to be precise. He grew up in a habitat that was formed in the years between the two wars; the factories strung out along the 'arterial roads', the Staines Road and the Great West Road and Western Avenue. Unemployment, in the worst of the depression, ran at five per cent or so; if you were a skilled engineer – and this, with the Midlands, was the territory of the engineer – you were all right. David Fuller's father was an engineer, and what excited him in boyhood was model engineering. As some men have sailor's blood and some railway blood, he had engineering blood.

He left school at fifteen to begin an apprenticeship with the British Thermostat Co., which broadened its scope and changed its name to Teddington Aircraft Controls. The apprentice became an engineer without any difficulty, and was soon picked to work on new developments in the company's experimental department. When the war came, he wanted to join the RAF but was already too valuable to be released. He worked on the prototype for a cooler thermostat fitted to Rolls-Royce engines, and then on developing a new kind of bomb-sight. So he might have continued, living at Feltham and working in the TAC factory at Sunbury-on-Thames.

But in 1946 the firm needed new and larger premises and the working of Government controls brought it to Merthyr. The management told Fuller that he was considered essential, and he made the move. Merthyr Council was anxious to make everything easy for new industry, and built a street of houses for key workers. Fuller got married and settled into one of these houses, with a view of the factory from the front living-room, and a shorter walk to work than most people have to the bus-stop.

He became a foreman, he became an assistant manager, and finally he became manager of the experimental department. This is the position he has held for the last fifteen years. At the peak of the company's operations, he coordinated the efforts of fifty men, all highly skilled and working individually or in small teams on development projects. He gave me a list of the projects for which he has been responsible, but in most cases the vocabulary would be meaningless except to the technically qualified reader. The last major job, however, was the throttle control for Concorde.

Short of moving to executive status, it is impossible for anyone in the enginering industry to be more important than in the kind of job that David Fuller held. It is impossible to be more completely the type of skilled, resourceful, experienced man on whom – so we are constantly told – the future of Britain depends in a world of sophisticated and competitive industry. When a firm wants to prove that it is doing a marvellous job and deserves to be admired and trusted by all, it pays for an advertisement with a photograph of a man like Fuller, if possible with a face like Fuller's. When businessmen argue that key men ought to be highly paid and lightly taxed (or else they'll go to America), men like Fuller are usually cited. Actually, Fuller's salary was £2,450; and if you know what salaries are in the entertainment business or Fleet Street or advertising, this leaves you wondering if anyone is at all serious about Britain's future and so forth. About that, however, Fuller himself was not concerned, or was too busy to concern himself. He found satisfaction in his work and he liked living in Merthyr; that was enough.

The satisfaction became less complete as TAC muffed opportunities and let projects languish, and Fuller is forthright in his language about the company's avoidable decline. In his position, he was not astonished by the final shutdown. But there was nothing that he, or any of the irreplaceable team of skilled workers, could do about it. By October 1971, he was unemployed. For the first time in his life, he is faced with an insoluble problem.

He would have been welcomed, or at least accepted, where the TAC work was to be continued – in Streatham and then, after the change of plan, in Yeovil. But Fuller whose tastes and habits remain resolutely working-class, has gone on living in his Council house. Councils nowadays don't provide houses for incoming key workers, and buying a house – that is, starting on a mortgage at the age of fifty-two – is out of the question for Fuller. Nor has the Yeovil firm offered him any help in that direction.

As he starts on the unfamiliar process of drawing the dole, David Fuller's financial position is far from desperate. His son is grown-up and teaching technical subjects in London, so he has only his wife and himself to support. Thanks to his long period with one employer, his redundancy payment amounted to what must be almost a record at £1,020, plus a commuted pension of £1,100. Still, the drop in his standard of living will be considerable unless he gets another job. Much more important, to his mind, is the fact that he enjoys working and detests idleness.

Accordingly, he has set out to find work in his usual

methodical way. At the time when I met him, he had written twenty letters and had six interviews. He had even applied for a job as far away as Maesteg, a nasty journey of thirty miles over two mountain ranges. So far, he has had no success.

There are three reasons for this. One is of a general nature – the state of the economy in Britain, and in South Wales especially. Another reason is that Fuller is over fifty. The third is that he never bothered to take any exams or acquire any formal qualifications. Initials after his name were not something he cared about. Now, he finds himself faced with application forms with a large space headed 'Education, degrees, diplomas, qualifications, etc.' After he has written 'Elementary school, Feltham' the space still looks large. Of course, he knows that he can do the job for which he is applying. But he can prove this only by doing it, which is a vicious circle.

What he thinks now is that he will probably set a time-limit on the search – he hasn't decided what the limit should be – and then give up. By 'give up', he certainly doesn't mean retreat into idleness. He has a hobby which could be an occupation; he makes reproduction antique furniture, with a special line in spinning-wheels. For a number of years he has had a workshop at the end of the garden. When I asked him how he fills his time since becoming unemployed, he answered: 'I get up at the usual time, I have breakfast, then I go into the workshop and I work like hell to stop myself worrying.'

It would be possible, he believes, to make a living selling this reproduction furniture. There are certain difficulties. He has yet to test the market or investigate the outlets, having made things only for his own pleasure and for friends hitherto; and affluent patrons, on the whole, tend not to live near Merthyr. Also, there is a rule against conducting a business from Council premises, so he would have to find a workshop and an office elsewhere. But these are problems to be solved. That has never worried David Fuller.

Britain, as a nation still loudly claiming a status in the industrial and technological world, can have either David Fuller as a development engineer or David Fuller as a maker of reproduction antiques. So far as he is concerned, Britain can let him know.

As I end this book, there seems to be no need for summary or the drawing of morals. A system that discards the men and women about whom I have written is a system that condemns itself.